THE SHRINK WHO STOLE MY LIFE

* * * * *

by

Jonathan P. Slow

and

Wilson H. Guertin

ALSO BY THE SAME AUTHOR

COMPANION SERIES-
HISTORICAL FICTION:
I, Joseph Father of Jesus. 2012. Amazon

I, Mary, Mother of Jesus. 2013. Amazon

Martin Provost, Survivor. 2014. Amazon

COMPANION SERIES-
EXPLOITS of the SEXIEST DETECTIVE:
The Sexiest Detective in West Florida. 2013, Amazon

The Sexiest Detective in Key West. 2013, Amazon

The Sexiest Detective in Ireland. 2013, Amazon

PSYCHOLOGICAL ANALYSIS:
A Desirable Killing and the Paranoid Mind. 2013, Amazon

CROSS-CULTURAL:
Beware the Beneficent Gringo! 2013, Amazon

Martin Provost, Survivor! 2014, Amazon

COMPANION SERIES-
SPY STORIES:
Istanbul's Silent Witness. 2014, Amazon

Istanbul's Secret Warriors. 2014, Amazon

Jonathan Padraig Slow, Exposed. 2014, Amazon

THE SHRINK WHO STOLE MY LIFE

by
Jonathan P. Slow
and
Wilson H. Guertin

Volume Two

This is a work of fiction. Names, characters, places, and incidents are the products of the author's imagination or are used fictitiously. Any resemblance to actual events, locales, or persons, living or dead, is entirely coincidental.

THIS BOOK IS FOR MATURE READERS ONLY.

Cover picture by Shutterstock.com

Cover by Bear

ЖК

Best

PSYCHOLOGICAL SERIES

The

FLORIDA
MYSTERY WRITERS

2014

To look for my happiness in the eyes of others, for my worth in the worth of those around me.

That is my faith, the inspiration of my whole life.

Michael Bakunin 1814-1876

TABLE OF CONTENTS

AUTHOR'S INTRODUCTION

THERE ARE many things about living that we need to learn. Often these points are best conveyed in the form of stories or novels. There is even a sobriquet with which to label them-- the "Cautionary Tale." The following narrative is such a tale.

"Fifty Shades of Grey" is such a novel and it provoked world-wide interest. The present volume offers a chance to look into the psyche of a different kind of a seducer, perhaps the flip side of Grey.

Not all dominating males act like brutes. The reader needs to recognize that there are other ways to establish male dominance. The subtle approach of the anti-hero of this novel is insidious because his type usually goes unrecognized. He exerts dominance by misdirection and passivity in his actions so that he seems to be a "Nice guy." He pretends passive compliance to give his partner a false sense of control.

This novel also contains explicit sexual content that some of you may find unpleasant. This does not diminish the book's value as a learning tool. In this tale you may gain understanding that will help you conquer the devil that lies in wait for you. You will see how your most modest sexual desires can provide the handhold for an outsider to manipulate you and penetrate your castle. Remember that disruptive sexual behavior arises because the normal outlet for expression is suppressed. If you don't believe me then go ask Freud.

Because of the potency of the content of this novel it would be well for the reader to keep in mind that the actual author is a professional clinical psychologist, publishing under the pseudonym of Jonathan P. Slow. Many years of his professional experience and understanding are concealed by his facetious pseudonym.

If you are involved personally in counseling, this book may trigger distrust and concern, as well it should. Determining the right to practice as a mental health counselor varies from state to state. There are no adequate national or state standards.

I wanted to dedicate this final book of mine to the very supportive and loving members of my family, and to Missy. They have helped me through all sorts of editorial problems and even technical and ethical ones. But my prim and proper wife objected to my acknowledging any family interest in the book. She said, "Your book is too disgusting!" So instead-- I hereby dedicate this book to my Puerto Morelos friends, Frankie and Paul. My children will sigh with relief to be excluded!

.

THE SHRINK WHO STOLE MY LIFE

by
Jonathan P. Slow
and
Wilson H. Guertin

REFLECTIONS

I'M JERRY. I'm the shrink who stole Jeanine's life, and made her like she is today. She's right, it was all my fault!

Father was right about me, too. He always said that I was a "Smart ass." I thought an education would put me above everybody else. I thought that I could manipulate the world about me to suit my desires. I believed that Bachelor-level psychology bullshit would give me the edge over others in the world. I thought I could rise to become "King of the hill."

Jeanine, my protégé sex kitten, who I created so proudly, is living contentedly in isolated rural Mexico with her girlfriend. My burgeoning career in business collapsed and I am alone and friendless-- I'm on the run and uncertain what to do next with my life.

I may have had a good run for my money but I was always destined to come to a bad end. Now, as a loser, I crawl to my former lover's doorstep begging forgiveness. I gave Jeanine the special gift of sexual freedom, but she accuses me of making her into the bitch that she is today. She screams at me, "You're, THE SHRINK WHO STOLE MY LIFE"

In my confusion I was wondering what I did wrong to ruin so many people's lives. I meant no harm, but I brought disaster! Now I was wandering around in rural Mexico trying to avoid the American arrest warrants with my name on them. OK, go ahead and name a charge and you'll find that there's a warrant with my name on it for committing that offense: Flight to Avoid Prosecution, Sexual Assault on a Minor, Operating a House of Prostitution, Kidnapping a Minor, Forging Government Documents, Resisting Arrest without Violence, Fraud, and Embezzlement.

To understand my life you have to realize that my actions always were based on one principle: "Do unto others as you would have them do unto you." A corollary to that principle is, "As ye sew, so shall ye reap."

No! I was not a seminary student! Quite the opposite-- I didn't believe in God and never wasted my Sunday mornings sitting with a group of superstitious morons, waiting for spiritual guidance from a non-existent "Father." As you see, my interest in scripture was purely lyrical because I was a practical, young man.

I was always nice to other people because that brought me rewards. I helped people feel good about themselves. I did things to please other people and society because it was to my advantage.

I was never troubled by a conscience that asks, "Is it the 'right' thing to do?" Instead, I would do what would profit me. My concerns were basic and concrete. Instead of looking for answers in profound philosophical areas, I would wonder if what I was doing pleased my friend and indebted him further to me.

I was a people person, rather than a science sort of guy. I enjoyed interacting with others and they, in turn, liked me. Many people thought of me as a friend, but I realized that I was my only true friend-- the others were just pawns in my boring life of chess.

I wanted others to like me so that they would do things for me, so I didn't disparage or disrespect others. I was what you might call, "A godless skeptic."

Such a personal philosophy can advance your interests but it also incorporates the seeds of destruction, just like body tissue may contain its cancerous enemy. So attend to my story and try to understand people like me. Be careful: We are charming, but we may be spreading the virus of your destruction.

PART ONE: Jerry in Atlanta

LIFE IN ATLANTA

MY NARRATIVE starts before I met Jeanine, when I was a piss-ant student at the age of 21. I suffered from the arrogance of youth-- it would be more accurate to say that others suffered from my arrogance. I had just received my Bachelor's degree in psychology and I thought I was hot shit! I was a bit of an embarrassment to everyone. In the year subsequent to my graduation I learned that my degree was of little practical value. Nobody had a full-time job for a wise-ass kid with a B.A. of any kind.

It was kind of late in my career to learn that four years of study only suited me to listen to selfish clients complain about their parents, or sit quietly while court-mandated delinquents cried about the injustices of life.

My first counseling job had been to monitor a hot line and tell the sweet young things on the other end that life really was good and that they should try to think positively instead of dwelling on negatives. I graduated from lying on the telephone to doing it face to face.

Now that I was employed as a part-time counselor for the city schools I had a chance to develop my "listening stance." While the client is bitching about boring details, your mind wanders, so you have to focus on something more interesting. As you might guess, my thoughts often turned to sex. Instead of smiling encouragingly I would be mentally undressing the female clients and ignoring the male ones. The girls thought I was kind of cute but the guys never seemed to form any attachment to me.

I'm a rather careful sort and like to avoid trouble. I would have loved to get my hands on one of the girls, who came in for counseling, but I was afraid of getting caught.

Grace had big tits and a nice body. She was good-looking too, but that was a secondary consideration. On Monday mornings I would review my schedule of appointments for the week. When I saw her name I would feel a definite twitch in my trousers.

I had mixed feelings about meeting with Grace. On the one hand, I couldn't wait for her to sit down in front of me and present her thinly veiled charms to my view. On the other hand, I was afraid that I might ruin my professional life and maybe even go to jail for making overt sexual advances. Hell! I wanted to jump over the desk and pump away at her, but I had to keep the beast in check.

Finally the time came when I found Grace so irresistible that she made me tremble from my impulses and I was afraid that she would notice that I was upset. She sat there smiling in front of my desk, while rambling on about her latest boyfriend. I sat behind my desk with a clipboard in front of me and I pretended to listen and make notes.

Temptation overcame good sense during one of her visits. I actually unzipped my fly with my left hand and held onto the beast that was trying to burst forth from behind the desk. I contemplated letting just the head peek out above the desk. Maybe Grace would be just curious, but she might feel too threatened if she were confronted by too much of a good thing.

I started working my left hand back and forth in a very slow quiet rhythm. The more excited I became the more I became afraid. As you know, fear has a devastating effect on the erectile function so I went soft as I was about to ejaculate. It was just as well because if I had come, Grace probably would have realized that I was masturbating, and there would have been a nasty mess of evidence at the crime scene.

I was in no condition to walk her to the door when she left. I mumbled a good-bye and couldn't wait to get back to the business at hand.

Grace never would know how close she came to being jumped that day. I was embarrassed by my loss of control. That incident betrayed how badly my needs asserted themselves and I was determined to develop a better approach for attracting girls. I became increasingly concerned; I needed to do something different before I got in real trouble.

The trouble was that I was falling into a pattern of perverse gratification. In the following weeks I repeated the fantasizing and masturbation during the visits with other clients. It was becoming a regular part of the office visit with a couple of my female clients.

I didn't feel guilty about viewing my clients as sexual objects but I did realize that what I was doing was dangerous. I found that my perverted behavior was much more gratifying than solitary masturbation. It would be hard to give up this exciting game, but I needed to break the pattern before one of the women realized what was going on and exposed me (no pun intended.)

I had been seeing clients for six months when it occurred to me: "I'm no good at applying psychology to my work, maybe I should change jobs." But entry-level jobs are had to find; I was lucky to have even this part-time job-- you needed a Ph.D. to ever get anywhere in my field. I asked myself, "Maybe you should change fields and do something useful like the medical technologists do." But I couldn't stand the idea of going back and spending another two years in college.

I thought, "Well, if I can't use my psychology to advantage in a counseling job then maybe I should seek some area where I could apply my training." During the subsequent weeks I mulled over my prospects. In short, I came to see little happiness in my future. I was not going anywhere in counseling and my personal life also showed no promise. If only I could apply my psychology to my personal life then all my study might not have been for nothing.

I was a twenty-one year old, horny bastard (as if there is any other kind!). Horny is good if you have an available sexual partner, but I didn't. The girls tended to avoid me because I took myself too seriously. I had two short affairs when I was in college but they didn't amount to much more than exploration and mutual masturbation.

My preference was for girls, but I found that my inexperienced approach to them prevented me from forming sexual liaisons. As an adolescent I played around enough with guys to learn that homosexuality was nothing more than mutual masturbation. Such escapades would not be rewarding enough to offset the negative consequences of such pursuits. So, as you see, I was living a rather sterile emotional life.

I was getting too old to settle for just the pleasures of the self-induced orgasm. I wanted some emotional involvement to perk up my enjoyment. That's how I was thinking during those dark days: "Spice up your life by applying some of the psychology that was going to waste."

So I started speculating about how to go about trapping and seducing, and finally training a female victim. I began thinking in terms of this being a spider-and-the-fly adventure, or even, as a psychological experiment.

I got very excited over the prospects. Yes! I would take my time and work the project over several months. I would use only sound psychological learning principles to achieve successive advances toward my goal. The idea was exciting, and I became obsessed with planning the details.

I even spent a little time considering the ethical aspects of the situation that I was about to create. I was doing the same thing that millions of ordinary guys were doing every day-- seducing and enticing a mate-- that's what life is all about. Look at the mating routines in almost any species of animal!

OK, so I was alright with the goals of the plan. Still, I was troubled by the violation of trust and responsibility that would controvert my assigned role. The client trusts the counselor, who has the responsibility to guide the client into constructive behavior changes. Was I ready to break that trust?

My answer to that was that I only would be helping the client move in the direction of enjoying a more gratifying life. There's nothing wrong with that is there? So then I felt justified in suppressing any qualms over malfeasance and abuse of my authority that seemed to be troubling me. After all, I would not being doing anything to harm the client; it would be a learning process and I would be helping her!

True, there was the small matter of my using my trusted job situation to my advantage-- to obtain readily-available sexual gratification. But what's wrong with enjoying your work? Why shouldn't I benefit from the fruits of my labor? These rationalizations were brilliantly conceived and provided me the reassurance I needed to go ahead full-speed with my nefarious experiment.

Still I could never quite resolve one nagging ethical aspect of the experiment. In the twentieth century there was quite a hullabaloo over small religious cults inducing young people to follow their "true" paths for reaching out to God. Their recruiting activities went by the pejorative rubric of "Brainwashing."

Brainwashing was severely condemned at the time. In retrospect I couldn't understand what was wrong with it; after all, the preacher was only teaching the client how to relate better to God. Were our missionaries doing evil when teaching scripture to black Africans? The parallel to my experiment was that I would be brain-washing the client to relate better to the joys of sex.

It seems to me that the difference between cult brainwashing and my familiarization techniques was clear. Brainwashing employed compulsive aspects, while mine were persuasive. Those thoughts reassured me and I just put away all those philosophical toys of childhood and went ahead with my adult pursuits.

THE PLAN UNFOLDS

SEXUAL relationships don't have to be toxic and I was setting out to demonstrate that. I was determined to set clear sub goals and never let my own personality dominate the direction or course of my sexual relationships.

Men often find themselves with partners who don't satisfy their physical needs. The woman-in-control often offers a man less satisfaction than can be obtained by hand. Unlike for men, sexual gratification for women usually is a very secondary consideration. Society marginalizes feminine gratification and men are so self-directed that they encourage women to ignore female needs. Too many women are left dissatisfied after intercourse and end up controlling the relationship as an unconscious way of manifesting their resentment.

Men work to their own disadvantage when they fall for the trap of feeling obliged to actively engage the partner, but then ignore her needs. They are led by their penises instead of by their minds. I was going to try to avoid making this same mistake. In all instances I applied the old British colonial adage, "Softly, softly catchee monkey!"

Already I was able to envision the results-- the passionate, loving partner that a man always dreams about, but seldom has-- a trained courtesan in his own bedroom. You might say that I was trying to produce a "sex kitten," or a "cuddle doll."

It was important to select the right subject. The first choice might not work out but I could find others if I were patient. I would look first for an attractive girl. A virgin would be best but an experienced girl would be OK if she hadn't been disgusted by her previous encounters.

It was important to find one, who had not been brutalized by men. The role she would learn to play would require her to believe that she was in charge of the relationship. She should not have learned to be intimidated into performing sexual acts. In short, I needed a malleable, willing pupil.

Fortunately there was an adequate supply of candidates available to choose from. The counseling center I worked for was a department within the local school system of a suburb of Atlanta. Teachers could come to the Center for a little friendly help in straightening out their lives.

The girls assigned to me expected to confide in me, routinely. I marked two of them as targets and readied Cupid's bow. I built a bridge to them by chatting them up, and at the same time found out about their qualifications.

I preselected the prospects by looking for a good, healthy and open affective response. I wanted a girl who was friendly and excited about life and would welcome new experiences. I avoided both timid girls and aggressive ones.

I took my time. After a couple of weeks I asked both of the clients, on my short-list, out for a cup of coffee. The next step was to meet them in the evening at a nearby bar to drink a couple of harmless beers together. One already was in a serious relationship so she fell by the wayside. That left me with one good prospect, Jeanine.

I never try to kiss girls seriously on the first dates. They are afraid of being hurt in relationships so they are looking for any excuse to terminate them before they become serious. Girls are all waiting for the guy to move too fast so they can protect themselves by rejecting him first. Some reject the guy because they are afraid he is too assertive and demanding. Others, who have been hurt before, reject the approach because they are afraid of getting involved with any man.

I found Jeanine particularly interesting. She was a year younger than me and was a generally happy person-- she was fun to be with. I told her what she wanted to hear before kissing her the first time.

I said, "I'm a little shy because I never dated much and I'm awkward around girls, but I'm comfortable with you. Would you mind giving me a little reassuring kiss?"

She couldn't say no without being rude. I got my first kiss but didn't push for more. I kissed her gently the second time when we said goodnight. My procedure and timing were directed at letting her think that our kissing was something she wanted and not something imposed upon her. Sluts may like rough handling but nice girls don't.

After the first date she kissed me of her own volition and put some passion into it. From then on, we started kissing more like lovers than like friends. It was still too soon to push personal intimacy, but it was OK to bring up sex in conversation, although I tried not to dwell on it. Talking about things is rather different that doing them.

Now we had reached the stage where we could talk about more personal matters. She told me a little about the guys she dated and what she liked in a guy. It turned out that she had been seduced by an older male cousin that she was fond of. They never repeated the experience and regarded it as an adolescent experiment.

I would be most reassuring and gentle as I listened to her reveal secrets that she had never shared before with a man. She told me about a lover she had two years ago. They were both young and inexperienced. She said, "I liked the sex part of it but felt he was too demanding."

I was careful not to let her tell me about one-night stands because I felt that she would be ashamed of them and then would hate me for knowing about them. I was learning about her personal life, but I had to share my own experiences with her to build her trust. I told her half truths but mostly what I told her were the things that I thought would be useful in furthering my goals. I fabricated my own background and history along those lines.

I told Jeanine how I had been raised up in a strict Catholic home, "I apologize for finding it difficult to talk with you about intimate things." She said she understood how it was hard to talk about them.

She assured me that she had done other bad things, but that she was embarrassed to talk about them with me. I didn't want her to feel that I was drawing her out, or digging for personal information. I reassured her that she was quite right to keep some things secret; she smiled at me and gave me an understanding kiss.

We had been going out for several weeks, long enough to develop mutual openness and a readiness to risk self-disclosure. I told her that my father caught me playing with myself when I was about 12. I explained that it all happened when my hormones were working to bring my body up to function at the level of manhood. I made up the story as I went along but kept it believable. She encouraged me, "What happened?"

I continued with my elaborate falsification…

"All morning I had been itching and burning down there. I rubbed it but I didn't know what was going on. It felt good so I rubbed it some more. Then I took out my penis and pulled it back and forth until it squirted out a milky substance. I was frightened and didn't know what to do. It was still hard and I had trouble tucking it away. Then father came in the barn while I was busy trying to clean up the front of my overalls.

He took one look at me and bellowed, 'Don't you know it's a sin to do that dirty thing you're doing?' I was too embarrassed to respond. He continued, 'You'll go to Hell if you keep that up. Go clean yourself up and change your clothes, but don't let your mother see your shame. Wash your own clothes and hide them away.'

You can imagine how terrible I felt. Would father tell my mother? I wouldn't have been able to bear it if she knew. I wanted to go to her for comfort but couldn't. I knew that she would be able to tell what I had been doing just by looking at me.

I skipped breakfast; I couldn't face the parents after what I had done. I was afraid to go to school because all the kids and the teachers would be able to see the Mark of Cain on my face. I was stained for life!

Father never brought up the matter again and neither did I. I told my pal Phil at school, and he said, 'Don't worry about it. It felt good didn't it?' I replied, 'Yes, but its wrong. It's a mortal sin."

At this point in my narrative I stopped as if embarrassed to continue. I waited for her reassurance and encouragement to continue. I wanted to maintain the fiction that what we were discussing was wholly because of her interest.

"Phil went on to tell me that all the guys play with themselves. He had been doing it for a year and loved it. He even offered to take me into the woods and show me how to do it properly. I was reluctant because my previous experience in the barn had scared the shit out of me.

The tie of friendship and recollection of the nice tingling feeling overcame my hesitance, so we went off to the woods together. First he took out his penis and showed me how to work it and then he encouraged me to do mine. I liked it. It was very naughty but maybe that was partly why it was so exciting.

Phil finished and then reached over to grab my penis. I asked him, 'How could you touch such a dirty thing? Aren't you disgusted by it? I don't want you or anybody else to ever touch it again. I'm never going to touch my own, never again, except to hold it when I pee,' and I meant it.

He ignored my protestations and pulled on mine a few times and I got all excited and screamed with pleasure. He asked me, 'Do you want to see me come again?' I was disgusted and excited at the same time. 'I guess so.'

He asked me to help him so I pulled it back and forth until he ejaculated again. He asked, 'Do you want to taste my cum?' I said, 'No.' I was afraid it was poison or would make me sick. I figured anything that came out of a penis had to be bad for you."

Phil did impart an important piece of information to me. He explained that his father had told him:

"Guys build up their juices, and have to discharge them one way or another. You'll come in your sleep if you don't have an outlet with fucking or masturbation.

The dream that accompanies the discharge is usually quite exciting. That's why some guys like to hold back the juices instead of discharging them by masturbating. They have great porno dreams in Technicolor but it can make quite a mess of the bedclothes."

I never did solve the problem. If I stopped the Devil's work, then I would be creating filthy messes in the bed for mother to encounter the next morning.

I continued my fabrication, as if reluctant:

"I couldn't sleep the night after my initiation into manhood. I tossed all night, sometimes rolling over on my penis. I promise you it wasn't intentional but I kept getting erections. Finally I couldn't stand it any longer. I sneaked out to the barn, uncertain what to do. I had avoided ejaculating in bed but now I was afraid it would come, all by itself. I just couldn't help myself. I took it out and let it hang outside my clothes in case it started spurting. I tried not to touch it anymore than necessary to pull it out.

Then I saw the rope and knew what I had to do. I picked up the one-inch rope and grasped it in my hand. I thought I was going crazy-- even the rope that I grasped felt like a penis.

I cried and begged the Lord to forgive me. I swished the rope to the side and snapped it back so that it struck my legs. The first blow surprised me. I didn't know what was going on. It should have hurt my shins where it struck; instead I felt relief.

I stopped trembling with fear and a different kind of feeling shook my whole body. It increased in intensity as I lashed my legs. I was so absorbed in punishing my body that I had forgotten all about masturbation. Suddenly, my juices squirted out and left me standing there in amazement. It was such an overwhelming experience that I thought at first that I was bleeding.

I didn't touch myself for almost a week. I could tell the juices were building up and seeking a way out. Sexual dreams increased in number and intensity, as did my erections. If I didn't masturbate in a rag I would have a wet dream in bed and soil the bedclothes, and shame myself with my mother. I was in a dilemma so I had to do something.

That evening I sneaked out to the barn and tried to squeeze the juices out, but I was too disturbed to get an erection. Then, I remembered how I had punished myself with the rope. I looked around and found it.

As I grasped the rope firmly in my hand my penis hardened. I fingered the rope preparatory to beating myself and my penis went rigid and throbbed with excitement.

As I struck my shins I told myself that I was evil-- a bad boy. I developed short panting breaths of excitement. After about ten lashings my penis shot its load without any manipulation. I cleaned up and went to my bed with a feeling of relief. I slept soundly, but I knew that the fluid pressures would build up again in the days to come.

For several weeks I used the lashings with the rope to bring me to an orgasm. During that period I never needed to soil the bed clothes, thank God! But I had become hooked on a sexual perversion and didn't know how I could escape. I knew that I would go to Hell!

I tried playing with my penis without the lashings but couldn't get an erection. Finally I realized that I hadn't masturbated successfully by hand in a long time. Perhaps

I could ejaculate if I just beat myself a few times with the rope to get hard and then finished off by hand.

I tried it and it worked. The first time I probably struck myself five times or so before it became hard enough and ready to ejaculate by masturbating. I found that I could reduce the number of lashings as I became successful in the combined effort. After two weeks I was able to get an erection and ejaculate by masturbation alone. I didn't need the lashings as long as I held the rope in my other hand and kept repeating, 'Bad boy! Bad boy!'

One time I went out to the barn and couldn't find the rope. Father had done something with it and I panicked. To my relief, I found it after searching for it high and low. As soon as I grasped the rope in my hand I started getting an erection. I was dependent upon it! I tried hiding it behind my back or burying it in a horse blanket.

Most of the time I was able to finish off without the rope, as long as I knew the rope was nearby. Then it occurred to me to cut a couple of inches off the end of the rope and carry it in my pocket. I even took it to school, snuggled up against my body, and that talisman completely cured my sexual impotence."

She queried me, "Did you always carry the rope-end when we first started going together?" I lied. "Yes. I was going through a period of feeling insecure so I brought it along for reassurance. I never really needed it though."

STRUGGLING WITH LIFE

JEANINE WAS such a good listener; she encouraged me to go on and complete my narrative. I was getting carried away with a creativeness and imagination that I never knew I possessed. I should write fiction novels. I reeled off my creations as if they really happened. I had finally found a use for the weird psychological case material that I had studied,

"I was a total failure. I had committed mortal sins and enjoyed them. I was so evil that I experienced sexual pleasure when I whipped the devil in my body. I hated myself and I hated my body because it was the home of the Devil. I despised my genitals because they were the cause of my downfall.

I wished father had punished me when he caught me playing with myself. Then maybe I wouldn't be out in the barn doing it again. He might even have castrated me and that would have ended my troubles forever. I even told Jeanine that I thought of killing myself-- that I deserved it."

I continued with my melodrama…

"I cleaned myself up and managed to stuff my offending member inside my clothes. Shaking with fear and excitement I walked up to the house intending to go to my bed. Instead I slipped below the floor level into the crawl space under the house, directly under my mother's bed where she would be sleeping. I needed her but couldn't go to her in such disgrace. I would never be able to look her in the face again. I lay there for a long time with the tears pouring out of my soul... I was exhausted but finally I turned my thoughts to comforting recollections of being with mother, I imagined I was lying in her bed and that she was cuddling me. I felt much better."

I interjected an intentional delay, "I really can't tell you what happened next-- it's just too horrible! You will hate me and maybe even be afraid of me." I made a sort of a sob and turned my head away from her. She reached over and turned my head back to her in an attempt to soothe me, "There's nothing you could tell me that would make me feel differently about you. I love you!" I yielded reluctantly to her persuasion...

"I slept a little bit after I recovered physically from my ordeal. I had calmed down considerably now that I was so close to mother. As I thought of mother sleeping above me I started to get hard again! What more could I do-- kill myself? I rolled on my side just in time to keep from coming on my clothes. What could I do? I was surely lost!

I crept back to the barn and told the Devil, 'This time I'm going to beat you until you are dead.' I started the switching and managed to get in a few swipes before my penis spurted again. I collapsed right then and there from exhaustion and surrender. I lay in the dirt until our rooster announced the arrival of morning. I pulled myself together well enough to be able to make it to school. I told my school chum Phil what had happened but all I got was, 'You're nuts!' "

I wanted to use "reverse psychology" on Jeanine so I told her that I hated my penis, "I want to tear it off and throw it to the pigs but I couldn't stand more pain in my body. If only I were a girl then I wouldn't have this ugly thing hanging down in front, creating all my troubles. I wish I were a girl with a neat little package there instead."

Then I turned to face Jeanine and told her that I was very sorry to have told her those things about myself. "You must think I'm a terrible person." I let her reassure me. She reached over and held me and then kissed me passionately-- but I moved slowly.

I would always be trying to get her to feel that she was the initiator in our future sexual ventures, and that she was drawing me out. We had reached the point where I could risk a slightly higher verbal intimacy level.

She was a woman and a teacher-- she was dedicated to helping people, and I offered myself as the helpless supplicant. It was time to bring out my, "wounded bird" ploy. I played my trump card:

"I couldn't tell you about my sexual disability before because I'm just not that bold. You've been so sympathetic about my problems with masturbation, that I feel that I can tell you anything I would tell a professional. I'm going to go ahead and tell you all my secrets, if you don't mind. The reason my two girlfriends left me was that they became impatient with my sexual problem."

I continued my fairy story…

"I suffer from erectile dysfunction and the cause must be psychological. At times I feel that I almost understand it even if others don't. I have never told anyone about it before, but I feel that you have a right to know. I realize that you would treat me with patience and kindness, unlike the others who focused on performance rather than the relationship. You are different so I'll tell you all about it, but only if you want me to."

She was sitting on the edge of her chair; of course she insisted that I go on!

"When I am alone at home I often get an erection while I am dressed in either street clothes or pajamas. When my penis is a little soft I rub it through my clothes and it gets fully hard, but just as soon as I take it out in the open it goes soft. Then it gets kind of hard if I rub it, but the erection usually doesn't last long. I can't use my member to pleasure a girl without it going soft and then I fail to come.

Instead of being tender and sympathetic, my old girlfriends used to get mad at me. I've learned that it will stay hard if I cover it with a handkerchief. It goes soft as soon as I expose it by removing that handkerchief.

Ever since my first disastrous encounters with masturbation, I have viewed my penis as ugly and dirty. The sight of it is disgusting to me, but you are encouraging and understanding. Maybe over a period of time I can change my view and attitude toward my penis. Maybe you can help me. I wouldn't be asking you to do anything sexual, only be kind to me."

I asked her, "Have you ever seen a man's penis?" She turned to me and said laughingly, "Of course, silly!" I pretended to be surprised. I asked her if she ever saw them when they were hard. She said, "Of course-- my old boyfriend's."

She continued, "Sometimes in gym an older student gets an erection and I have to pretend that I don't see it. It's really kind of funny." I chuckled with her, "That's what I like about you; you don't take things too seriously." I wanted to provoke her so I said, "You must think penises are ugly, don't you? I don't see how a girl could let a man come near her with an erection."

She reassured me that penises were OK, and that, "It's natural for them to get hard sometimes." I told her that I wasn't so sure. I had tried to get used to my own and to my friend Phil's, but they still looked like an appendage of the Devil. She asked me, "Where would you be now if your father didn't have one to use to make babies with?" I mumbled, "I guess so."

Jeanine took me by the hand tenderly and said, "I have secrets I thought I would never be able to share with anyone, but I want to tell you one of them, but you have to promise not to despise me." I told her, "There is nothing you could tell me that would turn me against you!" She snickered and replied, "We'll see about that."

"You asked me if I had ever seen a penis before but you were forgetting that I have an older brother. We used to sleep in the same room and I would see his little worm from time to time when he was changing clothes.

It wasn't of much interest until the day I saw him with an erection. I came into the room after school and he was lying on the bed, playing with himself. He tried to hide his indiscretion, but he knew that I saw him while he was busy at work. He was intimidated by being caught. He asked me, 'Just don't tell Mom, OK?'

I knew a little about penises but had never touched one. I was only about sixteen, but I was so naughty! I went over to the bed and reached out and grasped his penis. He didn't stop me so I just went ahead and jerked it up and down like he had been doing.

With a shudder he came in a rag and made me promise that I would never tell any one. I promised, but I made him make a promise too. He had to agree to let me do it again whenever I wanted to.

A few days later I went up to him and rubbed his crotch until it got hard. Then I knelt down on the floor and got him off. I used to do that about once a week. He loved it and never discouraged me.

One night when all was quiet, we joined up for a little play. I got so excited that I put his penis in my mouth just as he started to come. We were both surprised and delighted, but we were ashamed at enjoying such forbidden pleasures.

It's good that he went away to college in another state or I might never have been able to adjust to a normal lover. By the time he was moving out I had reached menarche and was playing with myself regularly.

I made him do me the final time that I did him. I loved the touch of his hands and the excitement they brought me. It was very hard for me to part with him. I was left all alone when he went off to school."

"I know you must think I'm an awful slut for doing such naughty things with my brother, but I couldn't help myself. I just loved his penis and how excited he would make me feel. Can you ever understand and forgive me?"

I reassured her that everybody goes through those experiment phases of sexual play. "It's no more wrong than riding on a see-saw board at the city park and enjoying the mixed feelings of excitement and disquiet in your groin."

She hugged me and murmured gratefully, "You're so understanding; I love you! I could never tell these things to anybody before, but now I am so relieved to be able to share them. I have another family secret that I have never told anyone about. Would it be alright if I tell you about that, too?"

I asked her if she really wanted to talk dirty anymore, "I just don't want you to feel that I'm forcing you to share your secrets just because I'm interested." Then I gave her the usual reassurance that she required but I noticed that she started reluctantly. I told her, "Maybe we should leave it to a later date. She scowled at me for discouraging her and began her account...

"My dad was pretty casual about exposing his body to the family. He used to walk around in boxer shorts and sometimes his penis poked its head out. He was careless of his appearance when he used the toilet or took a shower-- all of us were. We treated bodily functions as something natural.

I must have been about ten or eleven when I started covering myself modestly and noticed that father didn't. I became obsessed with watching for him to expose himself. One time I caught him stroking himself and it had grown to a frightening size. I sneaked away quickly, but wished I had stayed long enough to see more of the interesting game he was playing.

I arranged to be near him when he changed or showered but I failed to see his big penis again. All I encountered was the little one, and once I had seen it at its best I wasn't satisfied with less.

I switched tactics to spying on him when he was in the bedroom with mother. After two weeks of diligent surveillance I caught them in the act. Through the crack in the door I saw father walk across the room toward mother, who was lying on the bed naked.

Father stroked himself as he approached her so that he would be ready. I couldn't believe what I was seeing-- my father in full erection. I rubbed myself while I watched, but I was too young at the time to reach an orgasm.

Father climbed on mother while I poked myself, imagining that my scrawny finger was a penis. I was all a tingle! I had never seen anything like it! Mother clasped father and they rolled around and pumped. Soon they went crazy with delight.

It was over-- my dream was finished, my fantasy fulfilled. I crawled off to my bed, dizzy with the excitement and I lay on my bed imagining that father was coming into the room with his big organ. I fell asleep but had horrible dreams of being punished because of my disgusting desires.

I dreamt that a pony was chasing me across a scrubby field and was about to jump on my back. He had an enormous penis and I was sure that when he penetrated me I would split into two persons.

One part would be the naughty girl, who needed to be punished and the other was mother's little darling, who always behaved properly. The dream ended with the stud tearing me apart by penetrating me and then the good me emerged, released from my evil half.

I carefully avoided going to my parents' bedroom ever since that night. I got away with sharing the one exciting adventure and it was too much to hope to be able to repeat it.

I had almost forgotten about the incident until the next time I saw father running about in his boxers. I knew what he had under them and I wanted to share it with him. I knew it would never happen but I was tantalized by the idea for several years afterward."

She turned her head away, embarrassed, "You must really be disgusted with me-- I'm so evil-- I'm worse than a slut. Only a slut would think about having her father expose his penis and want to play with it-- yes, even take it inside her! I'm so ashamed. You must be disgusted with me." I gave her the usual reassurances so that she would feel comfortable enough to go on relating her secrets to me in the future.

All this sex talk was moving too fast and I was afraid that she would have a counter-reaction to making these revelations, but I couldn't get her off the subject. I asked her if it wouldn't be better to wait for another time for us to talk about sex.

She became angry and the corners of her mouth went down. She said, "Don't be such a prude! I might as well tell you everything. After my brother went away to college I had another sexual experience."...

"One of the kids in my class was kind of cute and I befriended him. But he was at the all-gonads age and that precluded friendly sentiments from entering our relationship. We were both about fifteen years old.

He kept pursuing me, saying that he wanted to kiss me, but I knew what he really was after-- I could almost smell the abundance of hormones in his make up.

One day I finally gave in. I missed the sexual experiences with my brother so I thought, 'What the Hell, let the kid have his bumbling way. It could be entertaining and exiting at the same time.' We walked down to the brook and hid ourselves in a grove of trees. I had already decided to give him more than he would dare ask for, but I wanted to string him along for my amusement.

First he asked for a kiss and I gave him a peck on the cheek. He complained that he wanted one on the lips. I pretended to resist but let him plant his eager lips against mine, and I had to admit that it was rather exciting.

I asked him, 'Can we go now?' He said, 'I promise I won't bother you about anything again if you just let me feel your breasts through your dress.' I told him that he was pretty nervy but that he could have a little feel.

He reached out for me with trembling hands and touched me gently. I pulled him tightly against me so that we would both feel the pressure of his hands on my breasts. He asked me, 'Why did you do that?' I replied, 'Because it felt good. Don't you ever do something just because it feels good?' He stuttered and said, 'Yeah. I play with myself,' I led him on by teasing him about being too young to masturbate. He said. 'No really, I'll show you.'

He proceeded to take out his cute little penis proudly. I asked him, 'Doesn't it get bigger?' He said mournfully, 'It usually does but I'm kind of embarrassed at showing you my thing.' I gave his little thing a few tugs and it got hard. Within a couple of minutes he had splattered the ground and was as happy as could be. He said, 'This is the first time I ever showed that to a girl-- it was great! Thanks!'

By that time I was getting pretty hot so when he wanted to touch my vulva I let him. I stripped off my panties and guided his finger to my labia, I told him to rub and he did so eagerly. He was working himself with his other hand while he was doing me. We finished and then packed up the traveling side show. It had been fun in a not-very-serious way."

I couldn't shut her up once she got going…

"The only other experience I haven't told you was about my PE teacher in high school. He was young and attractive so I set out to be noticed by him.

I didn't have any idea where it would lead but I hung out sometimes with him after school hours. He asked me, 'Do you know how pretty you are?' I told him that I didn't think about such things. Of course that was a lie. He reassured me that my awkward adolescent body was beautiful too. He flattered me and said, 'You'd make a super nude model.' He asked if I knew that he was a photographer. I told him, 'No.'

Then he planted the idea in my head that it would be naughty fun to pose for him in the nude. A week later he persuaded me to meet him alone at his apartment to have my picture taken. He was a lot older than I was so I was uncomfortable. He asked me if I wanted anything before we started. I told him, 'No. I just want to do the posing and with no funny stuff!' "

There was no stopping her once she started unloading her secrets. She continued:

"He seated me and brought out some pictures of nude males. I thought that there was something not quite right because the guys all had enormous erections projecting out from their bodies. I naively asked him, 'Do guys always get erections when they pose in the nude?'

He smirked and said, 'It all depends. Have you seen actual men with erections before?' I said 'Yes.' He asked, 'When?' I told him, 'It's none of your business!' He said, 'I bet you haven't, so I'm going to show you a real live erection-- my own!' He stripped off his jeans and his boxer shorts and proudly displayed his manhood.

I had to admit that the whole scene was exciting. He asked me, 'Do you want to touch it?' I was itching to grab it but was not ready to give him control over me. I said, 'My brother's is as big as yours and I can hold his anytime I want to. What would I want with yours?' He said, 'It does tricks! Come closer and I'll let you see.' I figured, 'What the Hell, it's sort of fun even though I'm not too comfortable with him.'

When I approached him he grabbed me and pulled my head down into his groin. I pushed away and could hardly breathe. He held my head down and stroked my hair. While he was doing that I was half choking and half sucking. He came and I couldn't help swallowing some of it. Out of spite I spit at least half of it out and soiled the couch.

He got what he wanted; he was happy. He had raped me! I hated him doubly because he made me partially enjoy the experience.

I told him that I would go to the police and report him if he ever bothered me again. He replied, 'I don't think so! You're not going to go around school telling everybody that you're an experienced cock-sucker! Besides you know that you loved it.' I got my fill of him and understood the expression, 'Be careful of what you wish for you might just get it.' "

I asked Jeanine, "Can we talk about something different?" She responded, "What's the matter? Does talking about sex get you excited?" She looked at my groin and smiled; I confessed that I had an erection.

She tried to reach over and touch my bulge, but I stopped her. I said, "You shouldn't have to touch a dirty thing like that." She laughed at me and said, "Don't be silly. If you can touch it, why can't I?" I persisted, "It's just not a nice thing to do." She finally gave up on me. I didn't want her to get discouraged so I reassured her, "I do want you to touch it but I'm too uncomfortable with that. Maybe I'll let you touch it some other time."

JEANINE CONFESSES

WE DATED for the next couple of weeks without sharing any more secrets about our naughty pasts. Things were going along smoothly and sex *per se* didn't enter our lives together. In the quiet of my apartment I was taking care of myself almost every night. Getting physical gratification was good enough at the time. I knew that she would be unable to postpone our sexual activities much longer, and I was waiting patiently

I knew that she had sex needs too and probably was playing with herself to meet them, while wanting to appear virginal on the outside. Now when we kissed it was for a much longer time, and the mouth action was more spontaneous and sensual. I knew that we were moving ahead because she held me tighter when we kissed and pulled me up against her warm body so she could feel my erection. I was getting mad with desire, as you can imagine, but I was determined to seduce her by capitalizing on her own desires rather than my own.

She asked me one night in the car, "When are you going to let me meet Mr. Johnson." I told her that we were waiting for the right time and place. She asked, "Can I hold him tonight, just a little bit?" I told her, "We should wait until we're more comfortable. I want you to be happy with me and Mr. Johnson. I don't want you to feel you have to do things for me out of obligation." She reassured me, "I'm just interested, and you never make me feel that I have to do anything for your sake." Those words were music to my ears!

I wouldn't let her have her way with me, until the next date. The next time we met she decided to entice me by telling me about some more of her sexual experimenting. She said, "You know, your penis wouldn't be the first one I've touched. My boyfriend lived with his parents so we used to make out in his car some of the time. He would take out his penis and beg me play with it. She continued:

> "I was bashful at first but I got so I liked giving him pleasure. I liked playing with his penis. I liked his penis and especially when he would come. I felt important to him, and for a little while I was in charge. I had him by the balls and could make him do anything I wanted him to do."

She smiled at me reassuringly and said,

> "You told me about how you thought penises are so ugly and dirty-- I never felt that way. I hesitated to tell you that before, because I don't want you to think I'm a slut. Actually, I think they're warm and cuddly, and very thrilling. I'm sure yours is too."

She continued,

> "I wish I had one of my own instead of a vagina. I only can experience the ejaculation of semen vicariously when it blasts its way out of the man's body."

I encouraged her to continue tantalizing and seducing me, and she did. "If you promise to let me meet Mr. Johnson tonight then I'll tell you a secret that I haven't even dared to tell my girlfriends." I agreed and she continued,

"My old boyfriend Jim and I were in his apartment celebrating his roommate's birthday. We were drinking rum and started losing control. Jim suggested that I give his roommate a birthday present he wouldn't forget.

The three of us got into bed and helped each other undress. Pretty soon there were two eager penises waving in my face. The roommate begged me to give him a blow job but I told him, 'I don't do that kind of thing, but since it's a special night I'll give you a one-time hand job.'

My boyfriend encouraged me so I grabbed his friend's penis and worked it the way Jim had taught me. It was very exciting and I was getting hot myself. Jim was cuddling up against me while I was doing his friend. When the friend came he communicated his excitement to me and my body conveyed it to Jim. Jim responded with a blast of his own."

She elaborated, "I may have only played sexual games with a few guys, but I realize that sex really is fun. I'll bet sex would be fun with you, too. I promise to love Mr. Johnson just as much as the ones I've played with before. I'm pretty experienced, you know. I bet I can keep it hard and make you come."

She blushed and turned her head away from me-- she couldn't look at me as she mumbled, "You must think I'm awful because I'm telling you these things. It's just that I want you to feel good about sex in general and your own, in particular. Now that you know all about me, how do you feel about me?"

I stuttered, "I think you're wonderful and I think I love you. I really do want to have you make friends with Mr. Johnson, but you mustn't rush me too much, OK?" She smiled her agreement. I smiled too; I love being seduced!

She really was just perfect. I wanted a trainee, who had not been intimidated by society into placing the whole sex scene off limits. At the same time I wanted a girl, who would be able to respond with initiative and not just submit out of fear, or because it was expected of her. She would have to become the leader and brandish a whip to maintain her position. I knew that Jeanine was the perfect choice.

We had Jeanine's apartment all to ourselves because her roommate went home for a week. Jeanine was rather uncomfortable and I behaved reluctantly. It was no accident that we were on her home turf instead of my own. I had planned everything so she would always be in charge and would take the responsibility for the fun and games we were ready to play.

She put on some records to play automatically and brought out some rum cokes to tranquilize us a bit. As we sat down on the couch I said to her, "This is your first chance to meet Mr. Johnson without anybody disturbing us. Do you want me to take him out to show you?" She conformed to her intended role perfectly, and said, "No. Let me do that."

I lay back and let her unzip me. She was talking while she was working, "You know, I think one of the reasons I went into Physical Education is because I love the human body-- yours is no exception. I love your chest and I love this little fella too."

Out he popped, right on demand. He was hard and getting stiffer. She looked up at me without releasing her hold. "See, that wasn't so bad, was it?" As she stretched it out from its hiding place she remarked, "My God! He's bigger that the others I've seen. You should be proud of him, not disparaging. Are you alright?" I grunted reassuringly and squeezed her empty hand.

She wanted me to tell her if she did anything sexual that annoyed or disgusted me. I told her, "You'll know that Mr. Johnson likes you as long as he stays this hard and ready to go. It's a sign that you're doing what's right."

She asked me, "Is it alright to make you come?" I wanted to blurt out, "Hell yes!" but maintained some composure. I replied, "It's your party, you can do anything you want to do with Mr. Johnson. He's putty in your hands."

She started working me up and down too fast. I asked her to slow down and to take her time in getting to know Mr. Johnson. I asked her to feel free to poke around.

Then she bent over my penis and studied it carefully. She said she had never seen an uncircumcised one before. "Would it be alright if I pulled the skin down so it will look like a circumcised one?" I reassured her again, "It's yours to do with whatever you please."

She traced the sperm duct by moving her finger up and down it. She was delighted when she noticed that the rubbing caused more juices to appear at the tip. She said with a sparkle of excitement, "That must be what it's like to milk a cow." I chuckled.

Jeanine played with some of the drops on the tip and asked, "Would it be alright if I tasted some of your juices by licking my finger?" Again I reassured her.

She was so turned on that she couldn't help falling deeper and deeper into the web of sexual intrigue that I was weaving. She already had told me that she used to take Jim's penis in her mouth when they were in the car and had no place to stretch out to have intercourse. She looked at me pleadingly and begged, "Please don't hate me for what I want to do!"

I told her, "There's nothing wrong with loving sex, we all do, and you're so good at it! I'll bet Jim loved what you used to do for him. Did you like doing it or did he force you?" She smiled coyly and whispered, "I loved it but not as much as I would if I could make Mr. Johnson that happy."

She had no intention of just tasting what was on her finger. She loved making her partner happy and knew that she was good at it-- she had a lot of practice on Jim. She gently took the tip in her mouth, but then she let it slip back out of her mouth and said, "You must think I'm just awful for doing this to you." Again I reassured her, "I love it please don't stop."

She lowered her mouth around my penis, and I held onto the couch to keep from lurching forward in heavenly delight. She retracted her mouth and looked up at me, "Would you think badly of me if I let you come in my mouth?" Before I could answer I was carried away with the release of my load.

She started to wipe the cum away from her mouth with her hand, but I grabbed her and pulled her lips to mine. I wanted her to realize that I would accept her sexuality no matter what she did.

I said, "You must be doing everything right because I have never enjoyed sex play like this before. Your love is working wonders. Look how hard I am. Thank you so much for being so gentle with me."

The reader may be wondering why I was so slow to stimulate her vaginally. Hey, girls like to be played with too, right? But they are protective of their bodies; once they spread their legs they become vulnerable. They are more secure playing with a guy sexually than by letting him manipulate them. That's why so many girls are "cock-teasers." Sure I wanted to get to her hotspot, but more importantly, I wanted her to lead me there.

She crawled even closer and snuggled up. She told me, "I have a confession to make." I acted surprised. She blushed and said,

"You're not the only one who needs to have an orgasm; I like to be masturbated by a guy. Even though I don't ever ejaculate I still need to experience a climax just as much as a man does.

All our sex play has gotten me so excited that I'm going out of my mind. I love looking after you and your needs but now I need attention. Please put your hand between my legs and caress my secret hot spot. Please work me gently until I come, too."

I replied, "That's the least I can do after all you've done for me tonight. I never touched you down there before because I was afraid you might think I was just interested in sex with you. I wanted our relationship to prove itself without having to depend upon sexual gratification. Now that we have developed a sound relationship I am ready to do anything for you that you desire."

She smiled at me and cuddled closer as my hand slipped into that warm wet spot that was waiting for me. I whispered in her ear, "Thank you for all you are doing for me. I love you!" Her response was a convulsion that almost bounced us off the bed. Somehow I managed to ride out the bucking bronco.

I lay back in the bed exhausted and went to sleep, but not before plotting the details of our next love-making session. For all I knew, Jeanine may have been making the same kind of plans. On my way home that night I was thinking to myself, "Wow! You never guessed that she was so experienced. She might be able to teach you a thing or two!"

So far, everything had worked out to be a win-win arrangement. She believed that she was curing me of my invented erectile dysfunction and disgust over sex, and I loved every minute of the treatment. I would be able to play a less passive role next time, but would be careful not to become pushy and threatening. She still had to believe that she was the one pushing all the buttons.

LEARNING INTIMACY

I APOLOGIZED for all the sex talk at our previous meeting. "You're a very nice lady and shouldn't be bothered about such dirty things as we were talking about. You're very attractive to me, but I don't want our relationship to be based solely on something like sex." She was a bit shy, "Oh, I don't mind-- I like talking about sex."

We went to see a movie together. She snuggled up close to me and put her hand down in my crotch-- she had already met Mr. Johnson. She reached across and kissed me on the cheek. Meanwhile she was undoing my fly and tugging on my penis. She leaned over further and took it in her mouth. After a few minutes she came up sputtering for air.

I wondered if the danger of being seen had contributed to her excitement and heightened the pleasure. This was the first real evidence I had seen of her exhibitionist/voyeuristic tendencies. Those interests could be worthwhile developing so as to include other people to enhance our sexual experiences.

* * * * *

The only thing we hadn't attempted was sexual intercourse. That was alright with me because I enjoy the foreplay just as much as the act. Later that week we took advantage of the roommate's absence and consummated our relationship.

As usual, I planned it so that Jeanine felt that it was all her idea. I let her get hot and bothered from playing with me and then I asked, "If you want me to do anything for you all you have to do is ask."

She smiled coyly and asked, "Are you ready to put that great big thing into me yet?" I told her, "Anything you wish. I will do anything for you!"

I asked her to get on top of me and lower herself down slowly on my erection. I explained that in that way she could take as much of it inside her as she wanted to. The idea of being in charge appealed to her. She was maintaining control and using me to meet her desires.

I reached up and cupped her breasts and she leaned back and let out a groan of satisfaction. I tweaked her nipples and she responded like a wild animal. She said, "I wanted you to play with them but I was bashful about asking you to do it. Oh! It's so wonderful." With such a responsive partner the mutual delight rapidly reached a peak.

We cleaned each other up as we climbed back down off the mountain top. We were all smiles. I lay back and she dragged her titties across my chest. Then she reached down to my penis and found it getting hard again. She said, "You don't seem to have any problem down there. We must have cured your sexual dysfunction. You've turned into a regular stud!"

By now she trusted me not to hurt or violate her; I wouldn't do anything that would spoil that trust.

She was completely vulnerable and I was her responsible master. I was her protector; she could always feel safe with me.

Mission accomplished-- I had trained my partner well to meet all my sexual needs. She had never been happier. Jeanine was an ideal companion so I invited her to move in to share my apartment. We were compatible in every way. I thought that we only needed each other until one day she burst that bubble.

WIDENING HORIZONS

JEANINE WAS a high school athletics teacher and she enjoyed her work. She especially liked to work with the young studs.

I thought that we had run the gamut of sexual games, but I was forgetting about the possibilities of including others in our activities. Jeanine came home in tears from school one day.

I asked her what was the matter, but all I got was, "I don't want to talk about it." But Jeanine trusted me; I was her only real friend. She was upset so I waited patiently for her to tell me what was wrong. It was an hour or so before she was ready.

She prefaced her account with, "Promise that you won't get mad and break up with me." I reassured her that she could tell me about anything at all that was troubling her. "I'm your friend and would never turn on you!"

She began, "Well, you know how much I admire human bodies and sex, too. I'm afraid I love sex and bodies too much. I'm insatiable and I'm in trouble because of it." I kissed away her tears and encouraged her, "Nothing is so bad that you can't share it with me." My kindly gestures only made her cry louder and the tears ran down her face. She blurted out…

"I've been unfaithful to you! I've been making out with one of my jocks and now he has complete control over me. He threatens to go to the principal if I don't meet him twice a week to give him blow jobs.

I'm sorry I created such a mess but it's just that I love sex so much that I couldn't say no to him the first time he suggested a rendezvous. He's a handsome hunk and I do admire his body, but now I hate him because he is forcing me against my will. I only want to be rid of him and be able to come home and feel safe with you."

I took a husky buddy with me to Jeanine's next meeting with the jock. We worked him over enough to get across the idea that his playtime fun had come to an end. I came back home and Jeanine washed away a little spattered blood and showed me how much she loved me. She promised never to cheat again.

But I'm a psychologist and a sceptic. You don't just wait and hope for things to happen; you plan the outcomes. I told her that the next time she was overwhelmed by her sexual interest in men, she should come to me.

I explained to her, "We can go over to the next town and rent a motel room for the night and then go scouting in town for a stud. Any pick-up for the night won't know us or our address so we would be able to shake him loose as soon as he fulfilled your needs.

She sat there in amazement. "Would you really pick up a stud for me to use for one night? I can't believe anybody could be as considerate as you! You're wonderful and I love you!" See. It pays to be friendly and considerate of others!

Everything was going according to plan-- I was letting Jeanine think that everything sexual that we did was to please her. It didn't occur to her that I like a little change too and that the thought of sharing Jeanine with another man was a turn on for me. My longer-term planning yielded tentative ideas of making the third person another woman instead of a man to share a bed with Jeanine and me.

One evening we went to the next town to try out our plan to share. Neither the stranger nor I were very focussed on the homosexual aspects of the encounter. We just lay back and watched the other working to satisfy Jeanine. While watching the scene of love we kept our hands busy with ourselves. I hadn't had any homosexual contact for such a long time that I couldn't remember what it was like.

* * * * *

We had tried everything and Jeanine was thoroughly seduced by this time; there wasn't anything sexual she wouldn't do. I taught her to look to me for all her satisfaction, but I never had guaranteed her loyalty to me. True, I had arranged experiences with other men so she wouldn't have to go about wondering what it would be like with a different partner. I just couldn't be sure that she wouldn't wander off from me. I needed to bind her to me by something more powerful than sex, alone. Fear would do nicely!

The next weekend I took a small, unloaded revolver along with us when we went scouting for a male partner. I left Jeanine in the motel room while I searched the bars for a connection. This time I wanted a guy for more than sexual play-- I wanted one to play-act, too. I searched until I found one, who agreed to act out a little farewell scenario with me.

We went back to the hotel and did our dirty deeds. About midnight he announced that he had to go home because he had to work the next day. As he walked toward the door he whipped out the empty revolver I had given him and pointed it at Jeanine. He told me to give him my wallet or he would shoot her. I pulled out my wallet as I walked toward him. I handed it to him and he pretended to make the mistake of reaching out to take it from my hand.

I lunged the short distance remaining and knocked the gun out of his hand. I picked it up and forced him toward the door. With Jeanine wild eyed, I shoved him into the passenger seat of my car. I told Jeanine not to worry-- to lock the door until I returned.

I drove off down the road and dropped the guy off near a bus station. The final action was for him to give me a bloody nose. After paying him off, I smeared some blood on my clothes and returned to the motel.

I reeled off my well-rehearsed story, "The guy jumped me when I stopped at a traffic light and the gun I was pointing at him went off. The bullet hit him in the chest and he died instantly. I just shoved him out of the car and came back here as quickly as possible. Get your things together. We have to leave as quickly as possible."

Jeanine started crying and couldn't stop. I comforted her and reminded that the killing was our secret, "Nobody saw anything or could know that we were the culprits. Don't worry; you have me to protect you." There we had it-- she was bound to me by the loyalty of spilled blood.

During the succeeding year, Jeanine only asked me a few times to take her to the neighbouring city for a fun-filled weekend with another guy in our bed. With successive excursions, the novelty was wearing off for both of us and so it became time to proceed with my longer-term plan.

* * * * *

I reminded Jeanine of my fabricated history of having difficulty in accepting sex as normal. We had cured my erectile dysfunction as evidenced by the strong erections that Jeanine still provoked. It was time to call attention to the fact that my successful activity had always been exclusively with Jeanine.

How would I do if I tried to make love to a different woman, one who lacked Jeanine's sensitivity and understanding? Was I really cured or would I go soft as soon as a strange woman made demands on me? Would I revert back to my earlier days when I was shamed before my two girlfriends?

Jeanine confessed being interested in looking further into my sexual life. After all, I had encouraged her to think of herself as my sex therapist.

She had been turned on before by sharing her bed with two of us guys. It was time for her to get used to the idea of sharing me with another woman in a ménage a trois. She seemed to like the idea of having a third party in bed with us, even though it was a woman-- or maybe because it was?

The next time we went to the city for the weekend, it was to entrap a female bed partner. I made the pickup alone so as not to scare off the prospect. The kind of girl I would pick up would not be very particular; she probably would be ready to accept Jeanine as a companion as well.

It really only required one trial to be able to demonstrate my adequacy with another woman. We made a few of these weekend trips even though we only really needed the first one. Strangers in bed can be quite a turn-on so there was no shortage of erections on my part. Jeanine proved to be a good sport and we took turns playing with this rented bed-partner.

I had to control my enthusiasm over these ménage a trois. I didn't dare let Jeanine know that I enjoyed sex more when we shared our bed with another woman. I had never reacted with jealousy on our previous expeditions to provide a man for Jeanine. I wanted to be sure that Jeanine didn't react jealously over our female bed companion, either.

We were experienced swingers and had proved that we could enjoy our sex wherever we found it. What more could I want? That should have been enough to guarantee a lifetime of happiness. I asked for her hand in marriage and she accepted.

MARRIED LIFE

ONLY AN extremely selfish man can ignore his own needs completely enough to focus sufficiently on those of others to use those needs to manipulate them. I am such a man. I spent almost a year postponing the meeting of my own immediate needs so that I could concentrate on training Jeanine. I had to be sure that she didn't wander off into the bed of some other rascal. It wasn't as though I hadn't had glorious pleasure satisfying Jeanine's sexual interests. It's just that I would have liked to indulge myself with a more spontaneous sexual life.

In the second year of our marriage my carefully orchestrated relationship with Jeanine started falling apart. She came home from school one day in tears. She said, "I've been very bad and I need to tell you about it before somebody else does."

"You know that I love teaching young children, especially boys. I'm fascinated by their innocence and their struggle to grow to manhood. What you don't realize is how much my concern extends to their fascinating sexual development too. But, even worse, I want to be a part of their sexual growth process.

Ever since the first days in my school I focussed my attention on one of my older students. I mothered him and looked after him. He trusted me and would do anything I asked of him. I seduced him gradually-- first by admiring his body and later by touching and rubbing it.

When he became old enough I took him to my car and explained, 'I'm so proud of you and I love your body, and I'm sure you are too. Are you proud enough of your body to show me your penis and how it can get hard?'

What horny 14-year-old could resist? During the second session he had a chance to show me his manliness by masturbating for me. You guessed it! By the third session I had his play toy in my mouth. This went on for about a month and I was fellating him at least once a week and I was loving it.

He told me about the things his best-friend classmate and he were doing to each other after school. I asked him to bring him along the next time we went 'for a ride.' They're so cute at that age! Everything went as I planned-- well, up to a point.

I liked my job and loved what I was doing. I never felt I was doing anything wrong. I was teaching the boys about sex just like you taught me. Of course I was afraid of getting caught but that's a different matter.

This went on nicely until the new kid told his father about our fun games. That father told the first father. At first they were both indignant, but they decided to handle the matter intelligently after talking over what they should do. They figured that they ought to get in on the games and so they came to me and demanded equal time.

I wouldn't have minded obliging them, but I wasn't about to be forced into it, so I refused. They walked out of the classroom saying, 'You'll be sorry!' Now, every day I go to school I'm terrified that the principal will call me into his office to explain what I have been up to."

I guess I wasn't really surprised, but I was furious that Jeanine had been so careless. I cursed her loudly for being stupid enough to bring such a mess into our lives. "I've looked after you in every way and made sure that you wanted for nothing, and now you turn around and do this? You've been lying to me and cheating on me. How could you repay me like that?"

I could hardly control my rage, "How could you do this to me. I gave you the security every girl needs-- I married you and gave you a home. We had a life together. You no longer had to worry about the future-- your husband promised to protect you and care for you. Why would you give all that up for a few minutes of sexual play?"

I asked Jeanine, "Why do you need such an assortment of penises to put in your mouth? Does that action replace normal vaginal sexuality for you?"

She obviously had thought a lot about the nature of her addiction. She must even have been reading Freud. She really wanted to explain to me. She pulled down a book from the bookshelves and opened to the "Oral Fixation" chapter. She said, "You, of all people, aught to understand my needs. Let me read you this reminder from your own textbook:

"Beginning with birth we associate physical pleasures with sucking. The nipple is the conduit to the world. At first we only have warmth and the image of a doting mother leaning over us to tempt us with an engorged breast. Is it surprising that this prototype of gratification continues in the growing child?

The infant focuses upon the mother's face, and she on his. Other parts of the body are ignored except when they become stinky. The infant's world extends hardly a foot or two away from his head. Anything beyond that has to be brought into his grasp. Give him a noisy rattle and he brings it into his world via his mouth. He is learning about the world that surrounds his head, and more particularly, his mouth.

He grows older and is praised when he learns to make a sucking noise we call a kiss. The target of his attention still will be primarily the mother's face. The face appears when he gets food or a dry diaper. Therein lies his source of security. He soon learns to suck his thumb or fingers as a solace when the teeth start tearing through the gums.

The mother's concern about eating comes later. She begs him to try a little food on a spoon and makes a big fuss over it. She gives him special treats and his love and appreciation continue to grow. Later he may go through a period of lollypop sucking. If he doesn't, then he probably ingests other candy. It's all good tasting in the mouth, and came from mom.

The mouth is the center of the face and he often focuses on it when talking with others. Why can't people see how important the mouth is?

When he grows older he misses his mom's nagging about his eating. For fun he goes out and gives his mouth a treat at nice restaurants. Some people are chefs, others are gourmets. Still, others just like to cram food in their mouths long after they have swallowed a sufficiency.

And throughout life he is trained and controlled by words from our mouths and those of others. Spoken words come to be as powerful as deadly actions might be. We watch mouths intensely while the words pour forth to determine our lives. Politicians use words from their mouths to send our youth abroad to their death.

When he reaches adolescence he experiments with smoking cigarettes, and perhaps pot. Chewing gum is available if he wants it.

When he is older he has lots of soda bottles to suck on even though all the nutritional sugar has been removed. He carries around his own water-bottle; he takes it everywhere. It's comforting to know that he can meet his oral needs immediately.

Later, he feels grown up and starts experimenting with alcoholic beverages. He swishes and guzzles them. Swallowing a glass of beer is not quite as satisfying as when he used to suck up a Smoothie with a straw, when he was a kid. Sucking on the neck of a beer bottle is more like it!

As he grows up it's time to experience some adult sex. It will be no surprise that the mouth and tongue come into play. He tries out kissing and finds it exciting. He used to like sucking and he finds that he still does; besides it makes two people happy, just like the old days at the breast. Unfortunately the sucking heritage persists with the male children too and they become conflicted.

Fellatio is not just a thing you do to a guy-- it' a very personal orientation to sex. You can feel the need to have a penis in your mouth for fun purposes-- just like inserting the penis in the vagina is essential for reproduction. If you learned to accept your body as it is, then you look for ways to please it sexually."

Jonathan P. Slow, 2014

She closed the book and looked at me pleading for understanding:

"My vaginal orgasms have never been exceptional; often I don't even come during intercourse, but you already know that. What you may not realize is that my mouth is my sensitive organ and my G-spot is there, not in my vagina. I am not like most other women, who require vaginal stimulation to reach orgasm. My orgasm is best triggered by having an erection splashing around in my mouth. Such an orgasm spreads throughout my body much more extensively than does a vaginal one.

When I am having intercourse I have a vague feeling of pleasure in my groin area. It feels warm and good but it lacks the sharpness and intensity of feeling of a penis actively moving around in my mouth and throat.

The penis in the vagina is remote-- somewhere 'down there.' A penis in the mouth is lively and playful. It demands close attention and never just lays there waiting for an orgasm to develop from somewhere distant."

Most women reject fellatio because it is too personal. Even prostitutes try to avoid kissing the client. The mouth is a very "up front" organ. It is impossible to ignore a penis in the mouth. You feel its every twitch and thrust, you taste every drop that leaks out, and you feel the warm gushes that the less-sensitive vagina fails to appreciate.

Women don't realize that the penis is the most precious possession that a man has. They fail to cuddle it and caress it with the tenderness and respect that it deserves. Despite all the kidding about it, the penis really is a man's "pride and joy."

Men shouldn't expect to encounter tender moments with a wife or girlfriend, who rejects a penis as distasteful. It's ridiculous to keep sex caged up, while exchanging septic spit with anyone ready to play kissing games.

STORM CLOUDS GATHER

I HELD Jeanine's quivering body and tried to reassure her. Three days had dragged on since the encounter with those two bastard fathers and nothing had happened. I reassured her, "Those guys are just hot air. They won't say anything because it involves them and their families. Just hang in there." I was wrong!

The next afternoon the two fathers showed up at our house. They acted threateningly and demanded to talk to Jeanine. I figured it would be best to let them clarify their position and then I would have a better idea of how to deal with this mess. I fetched Jeanine.

She turned her back to the fathers and wouldn't talk to them. She told me, "You can't make me talk to them!" One of them came over and stood in front of her face and said, "What's the matter? Do you only suck little kids' cocks? Are you afraid to do real men?"

I was disgusted. I had warned Jeanine not to get us into a mess like this, but she hadn't listened. I stopped being a sensitive, understanding psychologist and reverted to the role of abused husband. I felt vindictive. All this time I had been protecting her and she didn't appreciate it. She was an ingrate and needed to learn what it was like to be treated like a guy's bitch.

I grabbed her roughly and pushed her into the spare bedroom and then I turned back to the agitated fathers. I told them, "Go ahead. She's yours. Do whatever you want with her. She is no longer my wife!" They went into the room and I slammed the door behind them.

I went to my bedroom while the three of them were rough-housing together on the bed. I gathered up some clothes and things and stuffed them into a suitcase. I walked out the front door proudly, like any other incensed husband would.

Even at the time I felt that I was being a little unfair. After all, I had trained her to be sex tolerant. She hadn't done much wrong sexually; mostly I didn't want us to get in trouble with the law. Frightened society often metes out unreasonably long sentences for the smallest sexual deviation.

I lay in a motel room that night thinking that I was a moron, but I had a man's pride. I thought to myself, "Maybe she enjoyed being raped by those two guys. I was always gentle with her; maybe she needed a little roughing up."

I should have remembered not to let my own needs become paramount in deciding things. There was one consolation-- if all Hell broke loose, then the wrath of God and society would fall on Jeanine, not on me. I was wrong. When society gets perturbed about deviant sexual behavior they search out all perpetrators, even though they are innocent or incidental participants.

I reviewed yesterday's scenario as I lay in my bed in the motel. Where did I go wrong? Then it finally came to me-- that which should have occurred to me months ago. The whole mess was my fault. I ruined the cosy little game we were playing when I started putting my own needs ahead of hers. I had stopped being a psychologist and behaved like a stupid male. I switched roles to become an inconsiderate husband.

I should have realized how exceedingly fascinated Jeanine was with penises, especially those of strangers. She never denied that, but I should have realized how addicted she was because I made her what she was! She told me how much she loved the weekend trips when we went to the next town to hook up with a stud from a bar. I watched how much she enjoyed being in bed with those other guys.

How did I spoil it? I put my own needs first and thereby ruined all our work together. I should have protected her from herself. I should have continued cautiously finding men for her to toy with. Instead I left the procurement up to her impulsive whims.

I was blinded to Jeanine's needs for men by my desire for sexual experiences with strange women. I led her into this mess and then I deserted her when she really needed my support. I had invested a lot of time and effort in training her. We both deserved a happier ending than just drifting off on the run from the law. I considered the idea of locating her and re-establishing our home in another state.

I thought of retraining her so that she would no longer desire strange penises. I might be able to retrain her by using saturation and revulsion to make penises unattractive to her-- a sort of psychological castration. I might succeed and it might be worth it because I still loved her. But that retraining would destroy her sexual life, and we would no longer be able to gratify each other as before.

Then I remembered the serious charges that must lie behind the warrants we were escaping from. I wasn't about to go to jail for ten years just so I could spend my old age quietly with an ex-con wife. I talked myself out of the stupid idea of reconnecting with her, and went back to sleep.

* * * * *

A few years later, Jeanine told me what happened to her:

"I spent a desperate night in our home after the two fathers raped me. I needed you more than ever before. I depended on you and you failed me. Those two bastards went to the principal's office to register a complaint about me the day after they raped me. They backed each other's story so the police were called in and warrants were issued for my arrest.

I got scared and ran. I was afraid to go back to my school the next day so I packed a few things and went to my sister's house. She was furious when I told her that I was on the run. She let me stay long enough to get my affairs in order to arrange my escape to Mexico."

PART TWO: Jerry in Miami

SETTLING IN

"The Babylonians released King Jeremiah, and showed him great kindness, allowing Jeremiah to choose the place of his residence."

MOTHER WILL have a fit when she realizes how appropriately she named me. We were a Christian family and my mother liked the name Jerry. At the time it never occurred to her that she was registering me with the nickname for the Jewish prophet and king, Jeremiah. I left "Jerry" behind in Atlanta; all my new friends in Miami knew me as Jeremiah. I was determined to please the Jewish family of the girl I was dating.

I realized that I had wasted three years of my life in seducing and then being married to Jeanine. Maybe "wasted" isn't the right word, because they were the happiest days of my life. Now that she was gone I had nothing to show for those three years except for some memories of great sex.

What the hell! Lots of guys spend their whole lives in fruitless marriages and don't even have good memories. But I'm a very selfish person and so I was determined not to waste any more precious years of my life expecting a partner to love me forever.

I realized that I should ally myself with a well-to-do family since my work skills were not remarkable. When you go fishing, you might as well drop the line where the fish are. I decided to devote my life's efforts to improving myself socially and economically. I adapted the priories of my milieu and placed social and financial progress ahead of immediate gratification.

I met the 21 year-old Rebecca in a course offered at Miami-Dade Community College. We sat next to each other, and guess what? I conveniently forgot to bring a pen to take notes-- she lent me one of hers.

When we met in class the next time, she announced, "No. I don't have an extra pen. If you want the class notes you'll have to follow me home and copy them." I deliberately ignored the invitation. I was playing her like a fish. I wasn't going to rush things and risk jerking the hook out of her mouth by precipitous actions. It was all downhill after that!

She was a highly-skilled artist in the field of human anatomy-- a medical illustrator. We both had an interest in the human body but with somewhat different perspectives.

That month we went out a few times for coffee after class. Then our relationship jumped a notch and we were having drinks after class. We were already in the groping-around stage by the time we reached the evening-out-with-dancing.

I had hopes of making friends of her very successful family. A secondary priority was to teach Rebecca to be a suitable bed partner. She was anything but stupid. OK, a little naïve, but she could learn to enjoy sexual games as well as most of her "liberated" friends could. At least she would have a good teacher.

OK, so I was disappointed at having lost the ideal sex kitten that I trained to satisfy my every need. I realized that I could never expect to have such pleasures guaranteed to me again. Still, Rebecca seemed to have a natural talent. I might not be the guy with the biggest smile on his face but I wasn't frowning either.

I knew that liberating Rebecca wouldn't be easy because of the attitudes of her people. They say, "A Jewish American Princess never gives head unless she sees the sparkle of diamonds in advance." I would add to that saying-- "If you're lucky, you might hope that she would repeat the favor on your wedding anniversary-- the 100th one!"

This time I decided not to try to create the ideal partner; I wanted to put all my efforts into building my place in society. For those reasons I had to manage her sexually just enough to keep her contented and happy. I had to have a happy wife to testify to my social worthiness.

I asked her, "Do you want to go to my place to make love?" She replied, "I don't do that sort of thing with guys. I don't like to sneak around people's houses as if I were committing some crime. But I can give you a hand job right here in the car if you want." She had a practical orientation toward sex.

She did me and made a good job of it. I congratulated her on being liberal enough to pursue the pleasures that appealed to her. Within the week I found out that she knew how to do more than just give hand jobs. It was obvious that I wouldn't have to pursue a lengthy plan of manipulating her to meet my needs. I would let her train me instead.

Like most every other woman, Rebecca felt an obligation to perform the passive role of sex partner in the "missionary position." I avoided pressuring her for special favors. I assured her that anything beyond conventional intercourse would be a bonus, a gift of grace to her partner and would be well appreciated.

I never forced her to do anything that she didn't want to do, and I never made her feel obligated to perform for me. I convinced her that anything sexual we did together was because she wanted to try it or just plain, liked it.

I believed I had the right candidate for a wife, and I prepared for the long haul. I stopped casual dating and shucked off my few male buddies. I was on my way to a new phase in my life and I knew it. I was a disgustingly confident jerk and could barely stand my self. I knew that it was only a matter of time and I would have Rebecca eating out of my hand and all of her family cheering me on.

This regimen worked just as it had with Jeanine. The difference was that this time around I put less effort into manipulating my partner. I had sort of dedicated my life to training Jeanine and ended up with nothing to show for it. I told myself to keep cool and only relate to Rebecca in ways beneficial for building my new life. Sex had to be good for both of us, but I wouldn't let it be everything, the way it was with Jeanine. I had made the mistake of loving Jeanine and now I swore that it would never happen again.

Rebecca was rather a bulky girl; she had a nice body but carried a little more flesh than necessary. Her features were surprisingly regular, considering her Eastern European heritage. She was both attractive and easy to ignore. If you were on the prowl you would definitely notice her. If you had just left your girlfriend's apartment after a gratifying visit, you wouldn't notice her even if she walked right in front of you.

To put it another way, Rebecca was attractive enough to keep me aroused when I visited her, and musing about my social prospects after I left. She was bright and interesting. I delighted in planning the next moves to advance my position within her family. It wasn't long before my aspirations led me to think about intruding into the family corporate boardroom, too.

MY NEW FAMILY

ONLY GRADUALLY did I come to see what an amazing business Rebecca's family had assembled. Cohen-Saxs Enterprises, Inc. began to manufacture generic medicinal products in a converted clothing factory in a Miami suburb at the start of World War II. Money and power tend to become concentrated in enterprising conglomerates like Cohen-Saxs. This single company grew from being the exclusive supplier of aspirin for the US Army to being added to Fortune's Five- Hundred Companies list.

During the war they bought out competing manufacturers to eliminate competition. Soon they had almost exclusive control of the markets. Twenty years later they went public and sold corporate shares to acquire operating capital for further expansion and to dominate more of the market. They used that cash to purchase large blocks of shares in other public offerings of important pharmaceutical houses.

In this way the corporation was able to regulate production quotas for their own products and at the same time control even larger corporations by appointing themselves to their Board of Directors. In this monopolistic manner they grew to control production and distribution of an enormous part of the American market.

My new family was in the business of manufacturing and distributing over-the-counter pills and patent medicines. The aggressive management that resulted in capturing the pill market continued undaunted, decade after decade. The market was enormous and ever-changing, as well as burgeoning.

They offered pills for killing the appetite, for restoring the appetite, for burning fat tissue, for dissolving fat tissue, and even for converting fat tissue. There was little evidence that the products would produce the advertized results, but that didn't keep desperate customers from buying them.

Many of the new products were a flash-in-the-pan. They were fantastic sellers for a year or so, and then they just sat on disillusioned customer's shelves. But the company would reap tons of money before discontinuing distribution. They made sure that there still would be time to realize an enormous profit even if the U.S. government agencies stepped in to force a product off the market, and that usually required years.

More recently, the business was taking advantage of the hordes of customers trying to extend their lives and the life of the planet by consuming "organic" products. They even added exercise equipment to their offerings so that they could profit on those sales before the products were no longer popular and were consigned to rust-out in a corner of the bedrooms.

A smaller division of the conglomerate was already offering nicotine-free smoking devices called e-cigarettes. They were developing edible tidbits and smoking materials that might be promoted and evoke a fad. As recreational marijuana became legal they would be at the front with their fashionable ways to ingest it.

To the naïve person, "Bigger looks better," but therein lies the weakness of corporate enterprise. As they grow in size and scope, the management becomes more heterogeneous, and divided loyalties develop. Soon, the successful subsidiaries have outgrown themselves and have to be sold off as separates. Cohen-Saxs was reaching that point.

I would have been too intimidated to set out to hook up with Rebecca if I had realized how big and powerful her family really was. Two brothers and two sons-in-law still provided sufficient family power to assure loyal support for the patriarchal president, Rebecca's father. There wasn't much dissension going on until I joined the team.

The first level Executives were all close family. The patriarch's children and spouses filled all the critical executive slots of: CEO, Chief Financial Officer, Director of Operations, and Executive Vice President. They were thick as thieves and good at running the family business. They watched out for one another and made sure that their subordinates put family interests first.

The next lower level positions were the Divisional Directors, and they were many. The executives at this lower director level were selected for their skills more than their loyalty, although the later had to be unquestioned. Some of the incumbents were employed because they were distant relatives or members of other important families from their society. The directors of divisions had their own sphere of social activities that was distinct from that of the top family dogs.

When you don't have much knowledge or skills you have to get by on bullshit. I was bullshitting most of the time, but this family business was founded on bullshit and depended upon a continuing supply of it to be able to survive. I'm a pretty good bullshitter. I definitely had a chance to build a future there.

To climb the executive ladder you always have to appear ready to oblige your superior without sniveling. You have to stick firmly to your principles while kissing his ass. Advancement in business depends in part upon reputation and in part upon the company you keep. Nobody will ever think of you as a team player if you don't like other people, or are considered to be a loner.

I couldn't care less about other people, yet I consider myself as a "people person." I rarely enjoy others; I just use them. I couldn't be a part of the aggressive, young Miami business people without appearing to become one of them. I played handball with the guys and battered tennis balls around, as required. I joined my crowd in their pursuits of pleasure on yachts and in the bowels of popular nightclubs. I even bought drinks for the bar-girls and pinched their asses.

It wasn't enough to travel with "The crowd," you had to become one of them. This meant giving up your freedom and making a marital commitment to one of the ruling business families. I had smoothed off Rebecca's edges and found her acceptable as a life-long mate. In addition, I had "made nice" to the point where I was almost considered to be one of her family.

My prospective father-in-law encouraged me so much that I confessed my intention of asking him for the hand of his daughter. With a long face he told me that his daughter would never be allowed to marry a *goy* (non-Jew, derogative for Gentile). I explained to him that it was wrong to quibble over trifles of insignificance, when a couple loved each other.

I fabricated a family background to please him: "My mother was from one of the tribes of Jews and she married my Christian father, subject to the condition that I be brought up according to the Jewish laws. That's why I was named Jeremiah, after the Jewish king and prophet."

Rebecca's father lamented that my father failed in his duty to bring me up as a Jew, "What do you know about Judaism? Nothing! You aren't even circumcised, are you?" I begged him, "Don't make me suffer for the mistakes of my Christian father. I beg you to treat me as your son and grant me the right to live my life at your side as a member of your tribe."

He was truly touched by my pleading and he gathered me to him, "From now on you will live as my son, and no one shall dispute your right to call yourself a member of our tribe!" We drank a cup together to pledge the formation of our connection.

It is never easy for a father to give up a daughter. The situation had been fraught with tension; both of us were relieved. My new father-in-law-to-be took the opportunity to inject some humor and said, "It will be a novelty to have a family member with his entire foreskin intact!"

That wasn't quite the last of it, because any time one of my brothers-in-law accompanied me to the men's room I would notice him sneaking a sly look at my uncircumcised penis. I never quite figured out what lay behind their clumsy voyeuristic attempts. Were they entranced by the sight of an unsculptured penis? Or, perhaps, they wanted to be reassured that they were not losing their place of power to a real Jew with all the rights of his heritage?

I worked up my way to becoming worthy of marrying a daughter of the Jewish community by making painful visits to the Temple. The wedding day came and the rabbi bestowed his blessings upon us.

I had promoted my fraudulent life to the point that we received the best wishes of the whole Jewish community. It was a happy occasion. Even I enjoyed that day to its fullest. I got so carried away by the good will of the occasion that I almost forgot my selfish scheming completely.

The wedding reception was in one of the finest hotels in Miami-- incidentally; our company had a controlling interest in it. "One hand washes the other!" The "family" had to elevate pretension to its finest form that day. They had to perpetuate the myth that the untainted daughter of their noble tribe was about to surrender herself to the world through vulgar marriage. All should weep at the sacrificial loss of her virginity! Such bullshit!

I managed to survive the ceremony without throwing-up. I guess the stomach grows stronger as you get older because none of the guests threw-up either. We exited the party to our eight-passenger limousine.

Her thoughtful father not only had arranged chauffeured transportation but also a footman, so that his little princess wouldn't soil her hands with dirt when opening the car door. Never mind what she might smear them with on the honeymoon!

I am happy to report that the wedding night high-jinks went off very well. She loved what I offered and never seemed to be put off by a little surplus foreskin.

We played the dutiful role of an innocent Jewish couple. Rebecca even joked about putting out a bloodied sheet in the hall to announce the consummation of marriage. Only one thing stopped her from wrapping up her bridal bouquet in a bloody sheet and propping it outside the door-- we had no blood! I refused to let her punch me in the nose just for sentimental nonsense.

As I look back on it, I realize that life was going too well; it couldn't last, and it didn't. The last great sex I had with my wife was on our wedding night. It was as though, the fun disappeared and obligation replaced it. It made me wonder where the great orgasms went that she used to have. I wondered if she hadn't just been playing along, using sex as the bait, just to get me to marry her. I realized that she probably had faked most of her orgasms while we were courting, and I felt demeaned. I was supposed to be manipulating her, not the reverse.

I reacted to her diminished sexual interest by ignoring her. Shortly after the honeymoon I began withdrawing from her and she became more demanding and dependant. I couldn't stand her when she whined and pleaded. She became so desperate that she offered me blow jobs in exchange for my love. Our interaction became mutually destructive and ultimately drove me from her bedroom. I looked elsewhere when I wanted a satisfying sexual encounter.

Rebecca became depressed and developed somatic complaints when faced with the disgrace of a failed marriage. It was no longer a pleasure to come home and have to listen to her complaints. The more she bitched, the more she alienated me.

One time she declared her love in no uncertain terms, "Jeremiah, I love you so much that I can't stand the thought of being without you. If you ever leave me I'll kill myself!" No man likes to be enslaved by a threatening wife. Fortunately, things proceeded better in my business life.

* * * * *

In the early days I was an assistant to the Director of Marketing and Distribution. This was an important division because it was through it that the new ideas and products, as well as innovations, emerged. It was the sort of darling of the thinking members of the family. They pampered us so that we would have the right environment for birthing and succoring new and improved directions to keep our subsidiaries profitable. Our particular division cut across all departments and we had free access to them so that we could study their current practices and products and suggest improvements.

There were surprisingly few squabbling going on among directors and managers before I entered the corporate scramble. During the first year I bought department heads' friendship and loyalties by a most insidious and devilish device:

I would make friends of a manager and then find out who in the company he depended upon for support. Once I found that out, I would hint to him that his friend was betraying him and turning against him. I would offer sympathetic support, and the victim would feel obliged to turn to me as his friend in the future. All the department heads were in my pocket by the end of the year.

.

By the end of the second year I had accumulated the support of enough friends to make a successful grab at the very important position of Director of Marketing and Distribution. I pushed aside the incumbent, who hired me originally. Over a two year period I had been able to hijack all his friends. I was in! I doubled my salary and became eligible for big bonuses.

I wasn't ready to stop there. I should have been content, but that's not the way the game is played in that kind of a business world. If you stop to smell the flowers the next contender will roll over you and stomp you into the ground.

I was the youngest director in the company. The old guard would chuckle kindly, "He's sort of getting ahead of himself!" But I aimed even higher; I was determined to become the youngest member of the Executive Director family members.

The "Old Man" came to like me because I had spent two full years scheming to acquire executive support. The only thing that was stopping my advancement was the absence of a vacancy at the top.

Only a nervy bastard like me would ever expect to talk socially with these business lions, let alone become one of the pride. It was a pretty exclusive club, but I'm a very determined person, as you already know. During my third year I further strengthened my standing within the family circle. I had to be very subtle in redirecting alliances to my self by letting slip little rumors that I had "heard things" being said about them by their friends. These people at the top were not stupid, so I had to inch upward slowly.

The oldest son, in the family was named Sheldon, and he occupied the executive position of Director of Operations. That meant that I was taking on a very important cog in the corporation operations but also a senior member of the Cohen family. I was determined to make his position my own. I was still young, only 25; so what if it took me a few more years to attain my top goal? I was earning a quarter of a million annually in salary and almost the equivalent in bonuses.

I went on from day to day looking for ways to direct any snafu's that developed, over to Sheldon's desk. I became impatient and wanted his job so I managed to develop a believable frame of embezzling against Sheldon that would make him look really bad.

I was desperate enough to risk incorporating a dummy business in the state of Florida in Sheldon's name. I needed no more than a bank account and a mail drop location to carry out my destructive plan. I authorized a company payment of $100,000.00 for start-up expenses for this new company.

The check came to the temporary mail drop and I deposited it by mail into the bogus company's account with an anonymous, bank-stamped endorsement. Then I prepared a check to withdraw the cash from the bogus account by forging Sheldon's signature as President of the new company, and transferred the money to his personal bank account.

I had learned to be patient; I went back to work and waited. I had planted the incriminating bomb; now all I had to do was wait for one of our accountants or an auditor to question the purpose of the receipt and withdrawal in Sheldon's company. It took almost a year.

No doubt Sheldon noticed the $100,000.00 deposit to his account, but he had no way of knowing where it came from. I had covered my tracks. I was counting on him being too intimidated to bring it to anyone's attention. So, he had to wait around anxiously for something to happen with the hot money sitting there in his account. At year end it took a single day for our lawyer to expose what appeared to be his embezzlement.

The patriarch was shocked when the bad news finally reached him. He questioned Sheldon, but learned nothing. Sheldon went so far as to hire a private detective to investigate the matter independently. It was all a mystery. I was the only one, who knew for sure what had happened.

It would be more correct to state that nobody else had any *evidence* as to who had committed the crime. Sheldon knew on an intuitive level, or on the basis of the answer to "Who benefitted by the crime?" He was sure I had set him up, although he couldn't prove it. He was very disappointed that the detective never did locate any useful evidence against me even though Sheldon knew that I was the perpetrator.

The patriarch's decision was to demote Sheldon to the director level and fill his vacant executive level position with some new person. The Old Man studied possible prospects and then appointed me.

I had finally achieved what I had hoped for. On the surface all was smooth sailing. I hadn't realized that the bastardly frame up that I had constructed would blow back on me in time. I might as well have painted a target on my back that was labeled, "Aim here!" From that time on I felt that I was carrying a monkey on my back and feared retaliation from Sheldon.

* * * * * *

When you come to South Florida you learn quickly how the game is played. You must look wealthy regardless of your financial resources. You accomplish this in two ways: You buy a canal-side villa and you acquire a boat.

Both acquisitions must be beyond your station, which means, you go into debt well beyond all possible salvation. Then the rest of your life you will struggle against insolvency or, if you are lucky, you die young and leave the debts for your family to deal with.

There was no way I could escape the burdensome expense of this high-stake game. If I stinted, others would under-assess my value and treat me with disrespect. No sir, nobody would ever treat me like an office boy again!

To play this game you had to purchase a boat to reflect your station. If you were short in character or physical endowment then you had to compensate by adding one or more lengths of ten-foot segments to your floating acquisition.

If you had enough money to pay cash then you could get by with a 30' boat. If you didn't have the cash then you needed to purchase a 40' by taking a loan on it. If you couldn't afford the down payment on a 40' then you should buy a 50' boat with all the trimmings even if you have to go to a loan shark to scrape up the down payment.

You had to spend each weekend out on the boat even though it was uncomfortable; it was the *smart* thing to do. I invited colleagues and family out for fishing on Saturdays. I hated fishing but that was another one of my dark secrets.

Sundays were "families on the water" and I hated them even more than fishing. You might even say that, "Life has turned to shit when you would rather be at work than recreating with friends and family." But it was during the outbound trips with my boat that I felt a bit of fresh air and a chance to escape. I dreamed of sailing away alone and leaving all my commitments behind: No more squalling kids, no nagging wife, no fears of retaliation, and no pressures of work!

Ah! The outbound trip! In my mind I would run down to Key West and cross over to the Gulf of Mexico. It would take days-- and so what? You will have left all your past behind when you are escaping; at least that was my dream. I looked at the map. The only Mexican cities on the Gulf of Mexico, close to Miami, were Merida and Cancun.

I wondered what life would be like, living over there. Somehow it wouldn't matter because I would be escaping to a refuge. Under those conditions, any change surely would bring me to the good life-- an escape from a despised wife and her boring family. I promised myself that someday I would give up everything and live the life of a beach bum.

These thoughts were the musings of a rum-befuddled Gringo with too much time on his hands. There was no way that I could possibly foresee that I really would make Mexico my refuge. It was destined to become the only place that could offer me solace, if not peace.

* * * * *

Everybody loved me, and I was getting rich. This should have been a period of bliss for me. I told my father-in-law that I needed a long, restful vacation. I had been taking lots of trips without Rebecca, and she complained to her father about my neglect. He must have sensed what was going on between Rebecca and me in our marriage. But he was a wise old bird and realized that forcing people to stay together never brings reconciliation.

Rebecca may have known all about human bodies as a professional, but she didn't know how to hang onto her husband's. I was dying to get away. My father-in-law agreed that I deserved a long vacation. I was a little disquieted at the time by realizing that leaving Miami for a holiday exposed my back to Sheldon.

MY CANCUN HOLIDAY

WERE ALL the tourists blind? I realized that this was "The grand hustle," as soon as I stepped out into the Cancun reception lobby for incoming passengers. These local operators know how to play the game. But the irony of it was that I recognized that the hustlers themselves would be even easier to hustle. Gringos were less likely to believe bullshit than were the Mexican dispensers of it.

I was grateful to my subordinate, Luis, for arranging this holiday trip. He accompanied me to carry the bags and keep me out of drunken quarrels. Without him I would have had to deal with the unpleasant annoyances that plague the "Rich and Famous."

Luis was Mexican and too well-defined as a Mexican national to have the flexibility I needed in a regional director for our company. Alongside Luis, I was grooming a Cuban named, Marcos. Marcos was my real choice for Director of Foreign Operations but I planned to depend upon my Mexican friend for practical matters, for the time being.

Luis had the "in" with the locals, and Mexico was a populous country. Our sights were set a bit higher than just entering the Mexican market, but one could do worse. Luis understood the system of payoffs that rolled along and eventually would spit out the desired result. Nobody understands better than a Mexican about the under-the-table dealings necessary in Latin American. I would depend upon him completely when we were in the research and development stage. For setting up production in Latin America and promoting the products I would depend upon Marcos, with Luis as his assistant.

Marcos was Cuban, and as such, he did not have the close identity to a particular Latin American nation-- he could represent everybody, not just Cubans. Once Cubans are in the United States they disavow preconceived national borders-- they become "real" Americans.

The Cubans didn't have to overcome the yoke of the patron-peon relationship like the Mexicans; all the Cubans see themselves as middle-class. It only enhanced *Popi's* hero status if he served time in a Cuban prison for civil disobedience.

All South Florida would still be a backwater refuge for snakes and alligators, if it hadn't been for the influx of the energetic Cubans, The Americans never invaded Cuba successfully, but you can't say the reverse is true!

Cuban fathers expect their sons to spend their weekends in the Great Everglades Swamp, undergoing paramilitary training. Meanwhile the Cuban mothers manage the Latino homes, pretending that all their men are national heroes. The Cubans have all been taught to believe the most exaggerated myths about oppression since those disseminated about the European Holocaust. Both peoples think the world owes them a living.

It is important for a corporation to have directors, who have a little something extra to propel them. It may be resentment, feelings of racial inferiority, or physical inferiority. Cubans often have that extra something. They feel that the world has stepped on their toes and deprived them of their proper place in the world-- it makes them all the more determined to succeed.

Marcos would eventually become my Director of Latin American Sales. Luis would remain my field agent, and a good one. He was Mexican so he was not overly ambitious.

On the other hand, Marcos felt cheated by being born a Cuban because it had placed a ceiling on his advancement. With our company he would be able to spread his wings and present the picture of an executive concerned with all Latin America. His family was very proud of him and so were we.

Marcos time would come, but in the early stages I needed a guy like Luis. He had always been most helpful in teaching us about the Latin American community in the Miami area. He was the perfect escort for my visit, and for understanding the Mexicans.

Through him, I was able to become acquainted with the mentality of the local Mexican peasants. This peasantry was made up of former tenant farmers of small plots, and of wandering dispossessed Indians, who lived wherever they found themselves. In the previous three centuries the Federal Government colluded with the *patrones* to push these impoverished people off their traditional land so the rich could establish large farms and estates. The *peones* would remain alienated until they could be adapted to become a part of the modern economy.

Marcos was busy at work back in Miami, but Luis and I were exploring the potential of the Mexican market. Marcos was bouncing around the statistics that said that there was a huge untapped market for supplementary medicinal-type drugs in Latin America. We were examining that market close up.

* * * * *

The witch-doctors (*Curanderos*) had dominated the Latino health field all too long. Public health had not improved under their ministrations, so it was time to apply another approach-- we wanted a crack at it. Despite the prestige of being an American company, we wouldn't cure patients any better than the native dispensers of more primitive placebos and talismans, but that wouldn't stop us.

Our company strategy was to get rich before we were unmasked and recognized as being no different from the other scoundrels. Somebody was going to sell "snake oil" to the millions of people who had just enough spare change to donate their *picayunes* to the coffers of Rome. We wanted them to support our company's hunger for profits instead of feeding the Catholic bureaucracy. We wanted to help them overcome their ignorant ways.

Larger companies with reputable names were slow to move into the distribution of "off-list" substances to aid in treating some common conditions. Our corporation was ideal for creating the fountain of expanded distribution of medicinal, nutritional, and supplementary health aids

Our Board of Directors had shown time and time again that all they cared about was making money. We would sell anything to anybody as long as our bank of lawyers said that it wasn't illegal or likely to lead to large liability judgments for failing to meet promised claims. In simple terms, ethics *per se* were irrelevant to our operations. The Board attitude was simple, "If it will make money, then we'll do it!"

The only resistance I encountered was from my brother-in-law, Sheldon. When the other Board members came up with questions that I couldn't answer I could see Sheldon's hand in it. He was nice enough to my face, but I could see the hostility reflected in his negative manner. I knew he was whispering behind my back.

He was the one person in the family that I had failed to win over. Once I perpetrated the embezzling scam he knew I was the enemy. He hadn't been able to turn the family against me but I knew that he was biding his time.

* * * * *

We just couldn't go on ignoring the Latin American market for off-list medicinal substances. I was only beginning to see how big that market could be. We had not yet glimpsed the huge footprints of the dragon that was stalking that market.

My job would be made easier by our corporate ethical blindness. I didn't have to feel personally responsible for all the disasters that would result from misled consumers following our recommendations.

Here is a partial list of the substances that I thought might be most promising:

BULL
Macerated Penis for male Sexual potency
Macerated Testicles for male Sexual Potency
Macerated Scrotum for male Sexual Potency
Semen for male Sexual Potency
Powdered Horn as Aphrodisiac for both sexes

COW
Macerated Udder for Eating Disorders
Macerated Placenta for female infertility
Macerated Uterus to prevent abortion

RABBIT
Ground Epidermis for male Hair Restoration
Macerated Uterus for female Sexual Potency

SNAKE
Ground flesh for Attention Disorders

TERMITES
Ground whole insects for Strength & Endurance

ANTS
Ground whole insects for Social Conformity

HUMAN URINE
Male, for Potency problems
Female, for Reproductive problems

Many of the natural substances we would use are unappealing, even disgusting. I can tell you that all of them are processed to transform their character in a rather standard way. Each substance is ground up or minced so that it loses it original nature and identity, at once. Then the material is washed to remove mineral contaminants. A second process employs oxygen to kill any remaining bacteria or viruses.

At this point the substance is biologically pure and has been transformed from its original character. It is a new substance: "An aid to better health." It is packaged and sealed under sanitary conditions, ready for dispensing by your pharmacist or health store. If you still think these products are disgusting then, you ought to see the natural animal products that are sold in the street stalls in Bangkok!

We even assure the purchaser that the potency and effectiveness of these substances proved to be just as effective after processing as they were in the raw form. Many studies will show that the subjects benefitted just as much from the processed material as those receiving the unprocessed form. The casual reader will conclude erroneously: "Both forms were proved to be effective."

Questions about the feasibility of selling a new line of Latin Health Products were sure to keep arising. The most frequent question was, "Where would all the scarce raw materials come from?" Difficulty in finding suppliers looms rather large in a superficial look at the problem. The truth is that only very small amounts of active ingredients ever are used in final products.

Most pill makers of prescription meds put as little as ten milligrams of the active ingredients in a pill. If there are serious complaints about the ingredient being too weak to be effective, you can double the contents of each pill and release a "New Revised Formula."

The other procedure is to conduct research that shows that there is no advantage in taking a higher dose. You establish scientific trials with one group of subjects taking the single strength, and the other group taking double strength. Since neither group would be likely to show any change with our treatment, the results prove that, "There was no superior benefit to the users of the double dose experimental pills."

* * * * *

I was glad I came to Mexico! These Mexicans were good people. Don't be misled by their customs. You have to understand from the start that in Mexico *commissions* are paid instead of assessing standard rates for taxes and fees. Gringos like to demean Mexicans by referring to their commissions as "bribes." The commission is only a bribe when the money is paid to give you an *unfair advantage* over other people requiring similar assistance.

A commission is a payment for services rendered-- if the visitor feels overcharged then the Mexican would be ashamed. To save face he would be ready to assume a bar bill for his customer in excess of the total amount received from the client. Most of the Mexicans would put honor above profit whenever possible. But they are a practical people and might give priority to feeding their children over an abstraction like honor.

* * * * *

The second day we were in Cancun we went out to visit an Indian village. The guide in Cancun promised us an interesting day-trip into the countryside. He said that the village was dedicated to tourists, interested in hallucinogenic drugs. They told us that we could see demonstrations of drug effects or we even could experience those drugs ourselves if we paid the price. The town offered a complete collection of everything to delight the heart and lighten the soul.

Everybody knew about the dangers of exposing any of the large drug dealer's activities. The death of snitches was reported daily in the newspapers. Dealers were protected and those offering the protection were killers. Luis talked with some locals to check out whether this village tour was possible, and whether or not it was safe.

Luis explained to me that the Cancun area was relatively safe from drug violence as compared with other regions of Mexico. He said that if we were in Tijuana or Juarez he wouldn't let me cross the street alone at high noon. Cancun and the whole state of Quintana Roo were dependent upon tourism. What was good for tourists was good for QR; what was bad for tourists quickly disappeared.

Malefactors never assaulted and robbed tourists on the streets of Cancun more than once. The whole community would know who the culprits were and would help the police find them. Before the sun went down the criminals would be on their way to some interior province and never be seen again in the Gringoland region of the Caribbean. So far there was very little crime of any kind in QR. The visitor was safer there than in any part of the United States.

The next morning Luis showed up with a taxi and the special guide. After an hour's drive we stopped and were offered coffee at a roadside stand. A wagon path led into the woods and the local guide invited us to visit his village. Everybody was careful, pretending not to notice an occasional armed guard partially concealed in the foliage along the way.

Luis has a kindly manner so we were strongly welcomed by the village officials. The two bottles of Cuban rum that he brought as gifts enhanced our welcome!

The *cacique* (chief of the village) greeted us cordially and invited us to rest in the hammocks suspended between the tree trunks. He offered us enormous locally-made cigars and then asked after our health. He gave us tea after exchanging ten minutes of social niceties, and huffing and puffing the local tobacco.

Modest amounts of pot appeared after tea for our immediate use, but the cacique made it clear that they were not pot dealers. "We demonstrate its use to tourists but we are not suppliers."

He asked us if we would like to smoke pot in honor of our visit. If the pot was strong like the tobacco then it would impair our experience rather than enhance it. We declined the offer gracefully. The cacique spoke to one of his lieutenants, who requested permission to leave us.

He returned shortly in the company of a wizened old man with a younger assistant. The cacique introduced us to his *curandero* (medicine man). The attendant was his apprentice son, as would usually be the case. Then, an interpreter asked us if we had any illness that needed treatment. We thanked them for their kind concern and we moved along to the next treat after some more of the pleasant smiling that we had been using to serve as a common language.

Our hosts wondered if we had come to witness the trance of the curandero after he ingested the powerful hallucinogenic root, *ayahuasca*. They explained that visitors were never invited to try the drug themselves, because it was too powerful-- even dangerous. We declined the chance even to experience the ceremony this time, after we learned that the ceremony would last until well after midnight. We explained that we had to get back to Cancun by sunset, but that we would appreciate the chance to witness it another time.

I never did get back to see the curandero undergo the transformation that the drug was sure to bring. We had to settle for the following verbal account of how it is used and the kind of results that usually followed ingesting it:

"The drug hits you suddenly like a war club and knocks you down to the earth. Your feet are torn out from under you. You are so weak that you can barely roll over on your side. Your soul erupts from your mouth with a roar and a flashing of colors.

Time is irrelevant to the user, but an observer might have to wait hours until the user comes out of his trance. He will bellow and roar while being chased by jaguars, and he will try to escape by leaps and jumps as high as the tallest tree. He may be on the run in this kaleidoscopic jungle for hours.

The jaguar turns into the form of his enemy, and the sky bursts forth with sunshine. The gold of the sunshine changes color and he is captured in a swirl of bright blues and greens mixed in with the piercing yellow.

He is given the sight and understanding of the gods. It is then that he knows who has been harming him and his loved ones. He begins formulating a plan for revenge-- he has to counteract the power that his enemy uses to cast spells on him and his family. Hours later he falls into a deep sleep. When he awakens he is refreshed, but he is alarmed by all that has been revealed."

After listening to this account, we agreed that this drug wasn't something to play around with-- it was for professionals. Nevertheless, I promised myself that I would return one day to experience fully the other world through the aid of *ayahuasca*

.
They explained that they brought mushrooms from the Aztecs for use by the gringo tourists. The Indians in north central Mexico ingest the peyote mushroom in their religious ceremonies but it is not used much in QR by the Mayan Indians, nor is the effect as violent as with ayahuasca.

By that time it was forenoon and *chicha* appeared along with banana leaves, each containing a charred body. We guessed we were supposed to eat the animals and drink the liquid, but we weren't very sure.

The little animals turned out to be guinea pigs, a local delicacy roasted whole with most of the hair singed off. We choked down the burnt meat with the aid of *chicha*.

The chicha was an Indian beer made of corn. The best kind is produced in the home from masticated *yucca* root (manioc). I like to think that the chicha that we drank came from corn and was not the kind that is chewed-up-yucca-root, spit out into a jug by the lady of the house, and left to ferment.

We had a chance to try another, more popular Mexican type of beer called *pulque* It is made mostly from corn and Maguey cactus juice (as with tequila.) It was slimy and stringy like sputum and other juices that need not be mentioned. It didn't even taste good. The locals admitted that most of them preferred to drink it flavored with lemon juice.

Our trip finished after we picked away at some more local "delicacies." We dumped a half- tumbler of *aguardiente* liquor on top of the chili flavored food that we had eaten, and created an inferno. I went back to our lodgings with mixed feelings about our adventure, but I knew one thing-- it was very special.

During that visit I had a chance to learn about the customs and superstitions of the locals. Many of their superstitions probably depend upon the placebo effect. Placebo effects are wide-spread throughout all cultures. Even people, who are not very superstitious, respond to placebo treatments. Placebo treatment is based in two parts. First you must offer a substance that is exceptional in some way and it should have some physical or logical link to the condition treated.

Secondly, an authoritative person or group of people must declare that the placebo substance does ameliorate the treated condition. Notice I never use the word, "cure" in referring to our type of business products. We are not in the business of curing people, only offering them some relief. The powerful A.M.A. makes sure that criminal law preserves the distinction between *treating* a patient and *relieving* a client-- only "Doctors" are allowed to *cure*.

You can sell refrigerators to Eskimos if you can make them believe they need them. If these Indians believe what you tell them then they won't look for proof. If they trust you, they trust what you tell them. Belief is based in interpersonal exchanges of trust. You can keep on selling ineffective placebo treatments as long as they trust you.

Their village council has no committee insisting on empirical proof of effectiveness. Only when they lose faith in you and your promises are you in trouble, and then you had better run for the hills. Jungle retribution and justice are swift and irreversible.

I had no doubt that we would be able to sell all of our new line to these Indians. The only question we had to ask ourselves was, "Will the financial return be sufficient to offset the expense involved in developing new processing facilities?" I was convinced that the company should start developing the big push immediately. That's what I would tell the Board of Directors when I got back, and I could be pretty persuasive.

I would suggest the formation of a new division for our Latino products. When I got back I would assign our marketing research people the task of finding a suitable new trade name-- I suggested "Casero Latino" which suggests something Latino that is homemade or native. It turned out that my name wasn't a good one but it sure brought a lot of laughs from the Latino members of our home staff. They said that Casero Latino usually meant video tapes of Latino pornography!

THE MEXICAN RIVIERA

THE NEXT DAY we hired a taxi to take us along the Caribbean coastal area, named the Mayan Riviera, after the Maya Indians, who populated it in the old days, and still do. We wanted to visit a "Cute little drinking village with a fishing problem," named Puerto Morelos. It turned out to be the kind of place, which like Key West, deserved to be renamed, "Margaritaville." If you listened closely you might think you heard Jimmy Buffet singing his popular ditty about Margaritaville.

I knew right away that Puerto Morelos was a place I always could go and leave my troubles behind. That's no small thing for a busy, important man like me. Peace is hard to come by.

The goodness of the indigenous people showed through even though we were in a touristic region. They were more expressive than in other regions of Mexico that I had visited. You could tell when they were happy with their clients and when they could barely tolerate them. I concluded that the Mayan Riviera region was a great place to be.

Earnest Hemingway wasn't waiting to welcome us when we arrived, but Edouardo was standing in front of his world-famous Cantina Habanero. Edouardo was the owner and a very genial host. After a few beers we tried out his famous kitchen. It was no wonder that Travel Adviser awarded his restaurant the Puerto Morelos Number One award

127

for several years in a row. We had to agree with the praise being passed along by former customers.

Puerto Morelos Frank introduced himself during lunch. He was an expat American, who knew about nearly everything that was going on in the province of Quintana Roo. He wanted to be helpful so he asked about the nature of our business. His face lit up with recognition when we told him our corporate name and he avowed that nobody could be more welcome.

He explained that the Chinese were getting ready to invade Puerto Morelos in such a way that everything would be changed. They wanted to build an exhibition hall and warehouse, the second largest outside of China. The project was named Dragon Mall and Frank described it to us:

> "The scope of the project is so large that the life of everyone in Puerto Morelos would be affected. They are planning to build a complex that would hold more than 3,000 retail stores. Similar space would be allocated for offices and recreational activities. Warehousing for shipping and storage would occupy additional space. They plan to build a new village of 722 new residences for their employees."

Frank explained,

> "The influx of people will put enormous pressure on existing facilities.

Our quaint fishing port will be expanded and the roads overburdened by the pounding of the wheels of enormous trucks. There will be a flurry of land grabbing for commercial expansion, and new workers' housing. Mexicans will be unable to afford there own homes any more."

Frank thought that the scope of China's development would be greatly limited if the Americans could bring in some competition. He liked Luis and me and he said, "I sure hope you are the guys to stand up to the Chinese and give them some competition. At least that would give us locals some leverage to be able to restrain their environmentally-unfriendly efforts."

Frank warned us not to make approaches to government officials a "Do it yourself" project. "Only Mexicans know how to deal with other Mexicans." He gave us the name of a Mexican lawyer, Ramirez, who had been involved with the Dragon Mart negotiations from the start.

I told Frank, "When I get back to the hotel I will send a message to the Cuban, who works for us, and is our Latin America specialist. I will tell him to get in touch with the Mexican attorney Ramirez so that they can meet in Cancun after he receives my instructions. I wanted that meeting to be scheduled before I returned to Miami, but I had learned that corporate business can't be carried out by depending entirely upon one's self. I still hadn't quite realized how slowly business matters unfold in the Caribbean.

Frank was not opposed to development, he was just cautious. He had concerns that the project would affect all aspects of local life, some adversely. Frank started out being favorably inclined during the first phase of negotiations, but he found that he could not always endorse the acceptance of their proposals.

Government officials were currently reviewing the plans, and requests for construction permits. They were the people authorized to conduct such matters-- Frank was only a retired resident.

When Marcos came over for the meeting we could discuss alternatives. My thought at that time was that we might be able to share, say 10%, of the Dragon Mall venture and proportional space for our products. Or perhaps the Chinese would be agreeable to renting out that space to us on a long-term lease. I had no idea what to expect from a Chinese businessman; I had never before even met a Chinese gentleman.

We hated to leave the Cantina Habanero and go back to our hotel. The expatriates said good-bye and invited us to come back again. Edouardo and his wife Natty waved us on our way.

FISHING EXPEDITIONS

THE FOLLOWING DAY we hoped to go marlin fishing but the offshore wind was too blustery. We went to the harbor where we received the disappointing news. But as the saying goes, "Closing one door opens another." Anyhow, there would be other days for going fishing.

We went back to the room to relax and read for several hours in the hope that the wind would die down. At least the beach might become pleasant. The bathing suits started popping up on the beach as the day became more inviting. There is always an excess of babes at these Cancun resort beaches, and we put our beach chairs smack in the middle of them.

I noticed one girl in particular was twisting around and staring at me from the time we arrived. I pretended to read my book to stall off an encounter until I had time to get my wits about me. I had an uneasy feeling that I knew this girl in some other life, rather than here in Mexico; I just couldn't place her.

I could stand it no longer so I went over and stood above her-- introducing myself like a blushing school boy. I expected her to grab her belongings and dash to the *palapa*-roofed dressing room. She didn't!

She smiled up at me and offered her hand, "Don't you remember me? I used to work in the same school as your wife, Jeanine." I bought her a drink and we chatted. Then she told me that she saw Jeanine last year in a top-class restaurant on the island of Cozumel which was also on the Mayan Riviera, just an hour's drive, south of Cancun.

She said she was sorry she didn't go over and speak to her, but she explained that she had been afraid that Jeanine was on the run because of the felony warrants issued in Atlanta. If you're hiding out, then the last thing you need is old friends showing up suddenly and calling you by name.

Our mutual friend from Atlanta continued,

"I debated speaking to her there in the restaurant but thought, 'I'll just leave it to chance. I'll walk past her chair and see if she recognizes and acknowledges me.' She never looked up, but as I walked past her I heard a guest at the table address her as Katya. I hastened my gait and never went back to that restaurant again."

I pumped her for more information but she had none to give. I wanted to look up my ex, but all I got was the name of the restaurant. I sat numbly musing about fate. What was Jeanine doing in Cozumel? Was she on the lam there, or had she just come for a visit like me? I refused to let my hopes rise because I was sure that I would never be lucky enough to run across her again.

I remembered the good old days of my marriage, but especially the nights filled with sex. Those recollections made me determined not to leave a possible reunion to chance. If one person could find her by accident then another should be able to locate her with a systematic search.

My current life was ideal; why would I want to introduce a troublesome ex into the equation? I guess I was just being stupid once again.

The next day Luis and I were off to the Isle of Cozumel to try to locate my long-lost Jeanine, or Katya, as she seemed to be calling herself. We stayed over on the mainland beach in the new resort area, called Playacar which is just opposite Cozumel. We had a rental car and the frequent ferry service to Cozumel offered rapid crossings. Our circumstances were altogether pleasant.

I lolled around on the beach for several hours while Luis was searching over in Cozumel for Katya. The sun is hot down there and there is little natural shade. You can't stay out on the stark beach too long, so I made like a tourist. I drank Margaritas in the shade of a palapa-roofed bar on the beach when I wasn't splashing about in the Caribbean waters. All the pressures were off me, and I could concentrate on memories of Jeanine.

Jeanine, alias Katya, was well worth going to Mexico to find. I realized that I would never again encounter a sex partner like her. Why hadn't I tried to find out where she went when we fled separately from Atlanta? Why did I wait so long? I moaned to myself, "Yes! You're an idiot!" But then I argued with my self, "You did the right thing all along. She was wanted by the law in Georgia and could implicate you. You did right to keep your new family and business connections as far away from your felonious past as possible." But then I came back to what really counts-- opportunities for great sex! I said to myself, "Oh hell! We probably won't be able to find her, anyway!"

This was the care-free Caribbean. Enough of being sensible! I reassured myself that we would find her now that she had been spotted. I urged myself to be patient, "You're no longer a pimpled-face adolescent with hot coals in his pants!" It didn't matter what I told myself-- every hour I waited for Luis to return with news was agony.

It was almost midnight when Luis came back to the hotel. He found the restaurant where Katya often took her evening meals. He reported,

> "The maitre d' gave me very little help considering the size of the tip I gave him. He would have spit in my face if I had given him the usual table-service tip of ten dollars. He was reluctant to give me any information and pushed away my outstretched hand. I made a stern face and he relented-- his fist closed around the bills.
>
> I explained that all my boss wanted was a chance to speak privately with the lady. I asked if he would deliver a note to that effect. He agreed but warned me that Miss

Katya was a lady and neither he nor her other friends would stand for any funny business. I assured him that we were all gentlemen and passed him the note that requested a rendezvous in the reception hall of the same hotel for 1:00 PM the next noon."

I wasn't going to be the one, who went on a fool's errand, so I sent Luis to keep the rendezvous for me the next noontime. Katya probably received the note but had not responded. Luis waited around for two hours, passing the time sipping rum-cokes.

He came back that afternoon to tell me of his failure to set up a meeting. I was discouraged and at the same time eager to see Katya. Who did she think she was to make me stand in line with the other bozos? I tried to put a positive light on her failure to show up-- "She must be so overeager to see me that she won't deal with an intermediary."

. I wasn't going to sit around in our quarters like a sick schoolboy waiting for his beloved! I went over to Cozumel to the restaurant, and gave my own note to the maitre d'. Fifty dollars assured that my note would be delivered within the hour and that there would be an answer waiting tomorrow at noon. The food at the restaurant was appetizing but I had lost all interest in food. I returned to Playacar in a dither and swore when I finally got to see Katya she would pay for stalling me.

All this hanging around and accomplishing nothing was getting to me. I was used to giving orders to subordinates, who carried them out promptly. I was restless and needed something beside beach and margaritas to occupy me. I admitted that finally connecting up with Katya probably would fix me up just fine.

I couldn't be sure that Katya really was Jeanine. Our mutual friend from Atlanta might only have seen somebody that resembled Jeanine. I got a sinking felling in my stomach. I reassured myself-- Jeanine had such extraordinary pale green eyes that nobody else could be mistaken for her. Then the next day I saw her with my own eyes.

MEETING KATYA

AS THE MORNING lengthened I told Luis to accompany me over to Cozumel. We went to the restaurant before food service had begun. Even the bar was still closed. The maitre d' kindly prepared a drink for each of us to sip on while we waited. As he served it, I grumbled to myself that I would, "Shove my drink up the glorified waiter's ass" if he didn't make something happen soon.

Finally, Her Majesty showed up at quarter past one. She was dressed sports-formal, which is to say that the clothes were comfortable but revealing, and only could be purchased from an exclusive boutique. She was very masculine appearing; I almost mistook her for a boy.

She sat at what probably was her usual table, and she beckoned the maitre d' to approach her. They talked for a minute and then he came over to me, bearing her gift-- an audience with her Ladyship! I told Luis to wait for me at the bar, and accompanied the maitre d' to her table.

She smiled up at me, without rising, and held out her arms for an embrace. I felt the touch of our cheeks and I knew immediately that she was Jeanine. This was affirmed when she said, "Jerry! How I've missed you during the years we've been separated! Sit down and tell me all that has happened to you."

137

I recognized the big change in her instantly. She was still warm inside but it was overlaid by mature control. In those first moments I realized many things about her. I realized why she had not come running when I summoned her to our meeting. I understood why she had not jumped up to greet me. I also realized that my precious sex kitten probably was gone forever. She had become a mature lady in control of herself, *and me*.

I sat there quite dizzy and confused. My life was suddenly changed; this new world operated under entirely different rules than before. But worst of all, I knew that I had lost my favorite sex toy forever.

I was desperate to get back in touch with her, to share her life's experiences since we parted. I wanted to know what she was doing in Cozumel, how she managed to maintain herself. Did she have a regular job? She had become a stranger to me and I couldn't endure the psychological distance that separated us.

She never did get around to telling me about her circumstances-- she kept on diverting me back to relating my own recent history. She encouraged me to brag and I couldn't resist her lead. I was proud of my advancement from office boy to millionaire executive.

On my way back to Playacar I realized that she had told me nothing about herself and that we were as far apart as could be-- we were not even friends anymore. Friends knew about each other and I knew nothing about her. Shit! By encouraging me to talk about myself she had directed the conversation completely so that I had lost the chance to reconnect.

I pretty much forgot about business while the two day's dragged by, waiting to see her again. She invited me to dine with her and Pedro, her "protector," as she called him. I suspected that he was her pimp. As I was dressing to meet Katya I received a hand-delivered message.

She apologized and declared how disappointed she was that something had come up to prevent our getting together that evening. She apologized for cancelling at the last minute. This was all bullshit-- she was just manipulating me. I was pissed at being forced to face my indignity-- I was behaving like a love-sick adolescent. She made me wait around two more days for her to make time for me.

She arrived for our rescheduled dinner engagement and I was shocked this time to find her looking very feminine. Her attire was quite alluring, and the masculine character of her appearance had been transformed into an appealing feminine one. Even the sharp razor cut of her hair was gone, obscured by a long blonde wig.

I tried to draw her out to tell me of her recent history, but she kept the conversation banal. She no longer chatted freely because she had learned by experience to not expose herself and become vulnerable to others.

I had lots of questions to ask her but I started with a simple one. I asked, "Why do you call yourself Katya?" She replied,

"I was on the run and needed a change of identity. I always wanted a name with an exotic sound to it and I wanted to play games with the guys who are always sniffing around. Katya makes me sound like a high-class Russian call-girl, doesn't it?

For my first several months in Cancun I pretended to be a prostitute from Eastern Europe. You know how much I like sex. I just spent my time going from bed to bed enjoying that game. I was good at it and well-paid. When I got tired of it I decided to audition for the role of a lady."

She said that she had married one of the richer visitors to Cancun, but that it didn't last. I couldn't get her to reveal any of the interesting details about that marriage except to say that she had walked away from it with a reasonable settlement.

"I have the use of a friend's beach house over on the mainland at Playacar and have become a retired 'lady.' Most evenings I spend over here in Cozumel with friends. But I liked being alone-- you can get too much of people."

It sounded like she had enough money so that she wouldn't have to sell her body, at least for a while. I wondered if she had foresworn her enormous need for sex and now lived a reformed life. That would be unlikely, and certainly a great waste of talent. Maybe Pedro was looking after her sexually even though he was a lot older than those she usually dabbled with. I was recalling the age of those school kids she couldn't resist teaching about the joys of life.

I let my imagination run away with me: Maybe she was waiting for me to come back to her so we could start our lives over again. How I longed to be back in her bed! That first night I had to settle for a little good-night peck on the cheek.

GETTING HOOKED

I TRIED TO arrange another dinner date with Katya and she professed her disappointment that she was tied up with business matters pertaining to her ex-husband. I had extended my trip already and couldn't delay my return to Miami any longer. You can guess where my thoughts were as we cruised over the Gulf of Mexico on the way home.

No. I wasn't worried about the things I should attend to, like board meetings, and an increasingly-desperate wife. I was obsessed with Katya. How soon would I be able to arrange my next trip to Cozumel? Was Katya missing me and wanting me like I wanted her? It seemed that my cuddly sex kitten had grown claws and loved sinking them into me!

* * * * *

You may be wondering how things were going back home in my absence. All things rot if unattended-- my marriage was no different. Rebecca had upped her consumption of sleeping pills during my absence and made my sexual welcome-home-evening a horror. It started with her scattering her food all over the dinner table. Some of the food still adhered to her face as we tumbled into bed on a useless mission. I couldn't maintain an erection and she fell asleep. Welcome home!

I went through the motions of managing at work, but my only interest really was to return to

Cozumel. I thought that maybe a weekend out on the boat would restore pleasure to my life. It didn't I got drunk and became morose. Memories of the good times back in Atlanta with Jeanine kept breaking through the drunken haze. As soon as I got back to my office I had my secretary reserve a flight to Cozumel.

There were things to take care of in the office so I couldn't leave right away. Still, there was plenty of time for me to mope around and wonder what the hell had happened to my successful life. My desperate circumstances somehow seemed related to the past, but I couldn't quite see how. I had trained Jeanine to be the insatiable sex kitten, so how come I was the one so desperate for sex? I was supposed to be the ring-master, yet here I was, jumping through the hoops!

* * * * *

Luis, Marcos, and I arrived at the Cancun airport on time. We shuttled down to Cozumel in an hour and unpacked at our resort hotel. I was getting impatient with living in hotels, no matter how posh they were. This time I came prepared to remedy that inconvenience by purchasing a beach house; I had arranged a line of credit with my bank in Miami.

Marcos started arranging his business interviews but I took Luis with me when I went house-hunting. Cozumel is an island with limited space so new construction is very limited. Do you remember that Katya told me she lived in a beach house at Playacar? I sure did, and we headed there. Luis had the foresight to get Katya's address the last time we were in Mexico, so we went directly to her beach house. An attractive woman with a German accent answered the door and said that Katya had gone shopping in Cancun with a friend. While standing there I noticed that a neighboring house had a for sale sign on it.

We said good-bye and I walked over to the vacant house. Luis went to the house next door to inquire about the neighborhood. Vacation spots don't have neighborhoods in the traditional sense; they just offer places for people from various countries to spend holidays. Residents along that stretch of beach were all non-Mexicans, because only foreigners could afford to own beach property.

The owner of the house next door assured us that there were no problems in the neighborhood. "Only nice people live here." Of course, I didn't have to worry about the offering price for the house because I was a rich gringo!

Luis and I went to the address of the owner of the house for sale; he lived in one of the beach houses nearby. He was German but spoke good English. He explained that his aged parents had been living in the house, now vacant and up for sale, but they needed closer supervision so they moved into his home. That left their house and furnishings to be put up for sale. He indicated that he would prefer to sell the house furnished and that was just fine with me.

Luis went down to the government offices next day to start the paperwork, and two days later I had the deed and bill of sale. Back at the hotel, Luis, Marcos, and I celebrated with a bottle of champagne. I was now the owner of a Mexican villa and was an adopted Mexican *patron*.

I should have moved slower and sought Katya's approval before completing the house deal, but I was impatient. I wanted to impress her with *fait accompli* by the time we next met. I was doing things all wrong since renewing our acquaintanceship. What was the matter with me?

I was tired of being a "whistle-prick" suitor. I sent Luis to Katya's house instead of going myself a second time. She asked Luis to extend her invitation to dine with her that evening at her home. She didn't offer a rain check, so it was more of a summons than an invitation. I accepted. I didn't know what she was up to but I was afraid to start up a manipulative game of my own that I would probably lose. I was her pawn and we both knew it!

It was a quiet, pleasant soirée with just three of us. Her live-in companion, Berta, was the same lady I talked with on my first visit. She was a buxom Teutonic blonde of about thirty.

I sat there at dinner trying to fathom what kind of relationship the two girls shared. Were they lovers? Of course they were-- Berta had the figure of a dyke that would be wasted on men. Was Berta a reformed prostitute? I even let my speculations focus on the three of us making up a ménage a trois.

The longer I sat there carrying on a supercilious conversation, the more I wanted to know about Katya's new life.

Katya admitted that she had worked as a prostitute when she first came to Cancun. Was she still on the game? Would she accept me as her exclusive client or was she above all that? Was there anything she wanted that I could offer her? She had money and companionship, and probably sex. What more could I give her?

What about this Berta? Was she a dyke? Had Katya given up on men and gone Lesbian? Where did Katya's "protector," Pedro fit in? Was he a lover, a pimp, or just a father-figure friend?

I wanted to engulf myself in Katya's sexuality, just like I used to be able to do with Jeanine. This time I didn't know how to start. I found myself completely crippled. I couldn't play the game without knowing Katya's rules.

The only new thing Katya told me was that she was the caretaker of the house in which she was living. The owners only came down from Canada for a few weeks in the winter; they were glad to have it occupied the rest of the time. Katya was transformed into housekeeper and cook when the owners were at Playacar. I learned nothing more about Berta except that she was just a companion who came to live with Katya.

What I didn't recognize was that Katya was playing me to the max. She already owned the house she was living in, and she lied to me about nearly everything else. I found out later that this caretaker bullshit she told was just half true. When Jeanine first arrived in Cozumel she was the caretaker, but as Katya, she bought the house outright when she got her divorce settlement. That's as far as I got in pursuit of Katya that trip-- not a scoreboard to be proud of!

* * * * *

When I went back to Miami I found an even more desperate and frantic Rebecca. I wanted to start divorce proceedings immediately but I couldn't because it would destroy my standing in the business and in the family. I may have been stuck in the mess physically, but my mind was planning my next escape.

It was six months before I could get away to Mexico again. Luis had stayed on at the beach house in the interim and was able to supervise repairs, remodeling and furnishings. Upon arrival at Cancun I went directly to my new home in Playacar. I was surprised and pleased to find at least something going right in my life. I settled in for two days just to familiarize myself with my new home away from home. After that, my hunting-dog instincts came into play and I started sniffing and raising my tail. I was ready to go out and get some fresh meat!

Wonder of wonders! I found Katya at home and receiving. We sat in her garden and had tea. Berta served us but then left politely so we could speak more freely about personal matters. I decided to jump right in. I said, "Shouldn't we celebrate now that I'm a new neighbor?" She asked me, "How?" I replied boldly, "You could ask me to spend the night with you in your bed."

For a moment I thought she would slap my face, but then the darkness passed from her face. She merely said, "Do you think you deserve me?" I didn't know what to say, but I had unleashed her tongue by my boldness. She said haughtily, "I have Berta to entertain me sexually. I don't need you. I have learned to get along without men!"

That explained a lot. She was bitter generally about men and about me in particular. She had somehow moved from joyful heterosexual gratification to a Lesbian subsistence. I wondered if she found her new mode as satisfying as when we lived together-- I doubted it very much. I understood one thing and that was that I was going to be pushing a wagon load of shit uphill. The delightful, fun-filled days of the past were gone forever.

Then I wondered, "How much was left of the old Jeanine, who was so dedicated to pleasuring males?" I had to find out, whatever the outcome might be. Being an optimist, I could hardly wait, but some very realistic disappointments lay ahead.

Berta excused herself after the obligatory polite dinner conversation. As she left I thought to myself, "Berta seemed rather hostile tonight, as if she were holding a grudge against me. Well, with a prize like

Katya, who wouldn't be disappointed at being crowded out?" I only hoped that the evening would yield a bed with a hot, trembling prize.

Katya decided to give up resisting me. This is not to say that she decided to accept me. As I walked with her to her bedroom I felt the tightened grip and the cold fingers that told me that she had by no means, surrendered to me. I couldn't believe the difference that four years had made in her-- she no longer was the doll that melted helplessly to my touch.

I wanted to make love to the fun-loving Jeanine, but had to settle for this controlling bitch, Katya. There is no such thing as "bad sex," so all I can say is that we had an enjoyable night. It wasn't what we used to have.

HOUSE OF CARDS

I MAINTAINED hopes of being able to restore Katya to the Jeanine that once was mine. I used my psychological skills to create Jeanine, why wouldn't I be able to use them again to reconstruct her from Katya? Must Jeanine remain lost forever? That was the kind of thing going on in my head as we flew toward Mexico.

This trip I flew to the Cancun airport but stopped just long enough to recover my baggage. Luis was with me as usual. We brought along Marcos since he was exploring the prospects of doing business in connection with the Dragon Mart.

We all piled into a limousine headed for Cozumel. The bright sunny day was invigorating and our noon flight left us the second part of the day free. I told the driver that we wanted to stop in Puerto Morelos to visit an old friend. He twisted around in his seat with a grin on his face and said, "Oh you want to go to the Cantina Habanero, No?"

I nodded in response and that encouraged him, "OK! You must like *cervesa Mexicana*. No?" I tried not to be a wise-ass, but I couldn't help myself. I replied rapidly to his question as to liking Mexican beer. "No, I don't like it but, I just love sitting at the bar watching stupid Mexicans drinking themselves into unconsciousness."

He developed a blank look and managed to mutter, "*Que*?" I really didn't want to start a senseless argument so I enunciated clearly, "I love the beer and that's one of the main reasons I come to Mexico." He was able to follow my slower version and he broke out into a broad smile. He insisted on buying me a drink because, "You are such a nice hombre!"

About then Frank showed up and I excused myself to go over alone to consult with him. Not enough time had passed since my last visit for there to be any movement or approval of construction permits for Dragon Mart. Frank urged me to be patient-- the Chinese learned over the centuries to be patient; even modern Chinese businessmen will readily spend as much time as required to outlast any resistance. "In the end they win!"

I thanked Frank and took out my company checkbook to write him a check. I put in the amount and under remarks wrote, the word "Consulting." A thousand US bucks will buy a lot in Mexico, but Frank knew that it was like a flea's poop when placed alongside the Dragon Mart interests.

Frank asked me, "Do you know how large the families are of the people who need the little supplemental income we might give them?" I smiled at him and grabbed back the check. I replaced it with one for $10,000.00.

* * * * *

About half an hour later we arrived at Playacar and unloaded our stuff in my beach house. It felt good to have this refuge, it was a home all my own, and I didn't have to share it with family. We had a meal together in a nearby restaurant and then I telephoned Katya. She invited me for after-dinner coffee, which signified to me an overnight stay. Berta was gone so we were able to express our concerns and interests more freely.

Katya lead off with a blockbuster:

"If you are thinking of having me for a mistress you should plan on paying for it generously. The owners of our house let me live here rent free as a sort of charity. I have accumulated barely enough assets to provide income for my expenses.

If the house owners sell the house then I will have no place to live and my resources would be insufficient to let me purchase a home (This was a lie). I would have to go back to work, and down here that means prostitution. Besides all this, I would lack retirement support.

I would be ready to give up my present mode of living and become your mistress if you would be willing to purchase a beach house for me as exclusive owner. I am tired of being used. Until that time you should not expect exciting sex. Once I feel secure I will show my gratitude."

I took what pleasure I could get that night. It was good and bore a promise for the future. It wasn't my old Jeanine, but I was encouraged. I agreed to do my part in reconstructing Jeanine by buying a house for Katya to make her more secure and grateful. I left Luis behind when I went back to Miami. He searched for a vacant house that would meet with Katya's approval. Then he arranged the purchase and transfer of the house by making sure the deed was properly registered.

* * * * *

My world was like a house of cards, shaky and unstable. My relationship to Katya still had not unfolded enough for me to feel secure about the future with her. My marriage to Rebecca was shit-- a constant annoyance. My world was spinning out of control and I had just about picked up enough speed to fly into orbit when Rebecca had a lawyer serve me with divorce papers.

If Rebecca divorced me I would be up shit creek, with the family. I didn't know what to do. If the divorce went through then my retention as an executive was doubtful. The family never forgot a slight or ignored a chance to get revenge.

I spent my days sitting in my office just thinking about Katya. I would speculate about how far along the road I had come in recreating the old Jeanine. Could the gentle Jeanine of yesteryear ever completely replace the hardened Katya?

I considered the worse case scenario: Rebecca divorces me, and I completely lose the family acceptance. Then I would be unemployable. I tried to reassure myself-- Hell, I could take my money and run! I can draw my huge severance pay, start collecting company retirement benefits, and sell the boat. The total of my liquidations should provide me enough to live frugally in Mexico.

I could go live with Katya in the house I just purchased for her. Surely she would welcome me-- or would she? A sinking feeling of doubt hit me in the stomach. I got to wondering if it hadn't been a mistake to buy her that house without having any guarantee that I would benefit by doing so.

Well, there wasn't much I could do except wait and see if the "shit hit the fan." After two months of moping around the office I could no longer live with my uncertainties-- I took off for another quick trip to Mexico.

* * * * *

I was just settling down to sleep in my house in Playacar when the phone rang. It was my oldest brother-in-law Sheldon. He was raging and crying at the same time; I could hardly make him out. He eventually got the message across, "Rebecca is dead. She took sleeping pills right after you left for the airport. Her dying words were wasted on cursing you!"

* * * * *

I caught the next flight back and did what was expected of me, although I was walking around in a daze. You may think that things couldn't get any worse, but they did.

It seems that Sheldon had directed his private detective back onto my trail, again. This time they discovered that I had married Jeanine in Georgia and had never bothered to get a divorce. You can imagine how well bigamy went over with my adopted family!

It gets worse! Sheldon took it upon himself to tell his sister Rebecca that I was still married to my first wife. Of course the earlier marriage made her marriage to me null and void. She was already depressed and didn't need that added burden.

The family challenged Sheldon as to why he did such a stupid thing as to tell Rebecca about my bigamy. Sheldon felt too guilty to admit his own wrongdoing. He couldn't face up to how he had contributed to Rebecca's suicide and so he dumped everything on me.

I had displaced Sheldon from his executive officer position a year ago and he never forgot it. He had it in for me from the very beginning and that was part of his motive in telling Rebecca about the bigamy. He wasn't man enough to admit that his hatred for me was a contributing factor to his revealing my bigamy to his sister. It probably added greatly to his guilt over her death. Now a rampaging guilt had become mixed in with his personal mourning.

Nope! That was not the end of it. The three top executives of the company held a special meeting called by Sheldon to disclose, "Certain facts of great importance." My father-in-law chaired the committee as corporate president. Nope! It wasn't looking good for me. My only consolation was that I only could be made to face a firing squad once.

Sheldon set forth the evidence that it had taken a year to discover. He displayed the papers that I executed to establish the dummy company that was attributed to Sheldon. Documentary stamps were clipped lightly to the document to show that the required taxes and filing fees had been paid. This agreement was accompanied by an affidavit from a Miami judge declaring that the stamps had been removed under his order and submitted for DNA examination.

The DNA report attested that the DNA from the saliva from my coffee cup matched the DNA of the saliva mixed in with the doc stamp glue. The case against me was airtight. They had proved irrefutably that I had deliberately perpetrated fraud against a senior colleague and family member.

All agreed that they should deal with the situation *en famille*. They didn't want a corporate scandal so they offered me a position with a considerable reduction in rank. Any suggestions as to how to purge me from the company and the family would have been more than welcome.

That same day the corporate news release announced: "Mr. Sheldon Cohen has been appointed to the executive committee in the position formerly held by him. This will enable the present incumbent the time to work on developing some exciting new ideas that he is pursuing."

Boy! The birds came home to roost that night!

JERRY'S LAST TRIP

I WAS SO embarrassed at the mess I made of everything that I left for Mexico as soon as possible. I came alone this time because I didn't want to have my opprobrium rub off on my innocent associates, Marcos and Luis. Besides, I was becoming physically afraid of strangers and friends, alike-- you never can tell what some people might do for money. I was afraid to go out in public places without constantly turning looking behind me and in the shadows. Maybe I should have brought somebody with me to watch my back.

Normally, Customs and Immigration took less than half an hour to finish; this time they stopped me at Immigration. I was not surprised. In this digital age the police get a warrant issued almost before the perp commits a crime. There must have been a bunch of unserved warrants waiting for me back in Miami with apprehension notices sent out to the Mexican police. I wondered if the charges were serious enough to lead to extradition against my will. I guessed I would find out soon enough.

When you are in trouble it's helpful to have someone to share with. I wished I had brought Luis along; he would have been able to assess the advisability of offering a bribe. When this official rousted me-- I hadn't any idea what to do, so I just sat in the chair like they told me to do.

After half an hour a polite official approached me and spoke to me in English. He apologized for the delay and explained that it was not their fault, "You are on the Gringo 'no fly' list, Senor." That was it; they caught me! I asked politely, "Can you tell me why I am on the list?" I figured he was going to delight in running down the list of crimes I was wanted for.

He said, "They tell us nothing. The list just means that you are a security risk." I asked him, "Why didn't the Americans stop me from flying from Miami if I am on their no fly list?" "I don't know Senior. You would have to ask them." He excused himself to return to his desk in the interior.

Half an hour later the same official approached me; he was all smiles. What did his smile mean? Was he happy that he had apprehended a master criminal, or had somebody just given him a huge bribe to release me?

"I have good news for you, Senior. The problem proved to be a mistake in identity. We sent a copy of your passport to Homeland Security in Washington; they couldn't find you on any of their lists so they said that it was alright to let you fly. It probably was just a mix-up in names."

I started to complain that I had just arrived; that the Americans could have no reason to delay my entry into Mexico. *I was arriving*, not intending to fly from the airport. On brief reflection I remembered that I was in no position to be creating a fuss with any type of official. A criminal like me should be grateful for being allowed to walk the streets freely.

The limousine was waiting for me to take me to Puerto Morelos. I arrived just after lunchtime and was looking forward to having tacos at the Cantina Habanero-- they have the best fish tacos around. The few diners, who were still there, were finishing up and leaving; the drinking crowd had not yet arrived. I enjoyed a nice chat with the waitress, Heidi. She, along with the barman, Roberto are always ready to assurer patrons that everything will look better tomorrow,

* * * * *

After settling into my Playacar house I went directly to the nearest bank and opened the necessary accounts. I had brought the essential financial documents with me from Miami, so that I would be able to access all the assets that I had left back there. Needless to say, I was welcomed because I was making quite a sizable deposit.

* * * * *

It was a warm moonlit night and I enjoyed the limousine ride to the restaurant. I lay back trying to con myself into believing everything was alright. Shortly I would be with Katya and she would help me get over the rough spots. I told myself, "You could even stay down here in Mexico instead of going back to Miami to face your messes."

You see things differently when you are down in the sunny Caribbean. Katya and I had a very nice meal and then we went back to her beach house to make love. I was telling myself that I had been making too much of my misfortunes.

Katya offered me an after dinner cordial and we sat quietly in the living room so we could enjoy it. After all, we had the whole night ahead of us; at least I thought we had.

Look at things from an optimistic point of view: I had a nice cozy place to live, down in Mexico-- I assumed that Katya would let me stay with her. I had income from retirement, severance, house rental, and company stock dividends. I even had the stock and the dividends from Rebecca's stock which I had inherited after her suicide.

The family had tried to keep me from inheriting her stock as her husband, because my marriage to Rebecca was voided automatically because of the bigamy. They found that they might be able to keep the *husband* from inheriting, but not the *person*, since she specified me by name in her will.

I remember a knock on the door interrupting the flow of our casual conversation. Katya answered the door and I heard the angry voice of my brother-in-law, Sheldon.

What was he doing here? He was supposed to be back in Miami. I got up to meet him and the next thing I remember I was laying flattened out on the floor with Sheldon's angry face above mine, while his knees pinned me to the floor. He was swearing and shouting at me: "How did you ever expect to pull all that shit and walk away from it? Do you think you can leave all your shit behind and come down here and live a life of milk and honey?"

The last thing I remember was that I could hardly breathe with all his weight on top of me. I felt his hands around my neck as I started to pass out. That's all I remember.

PART THREE: Kitty in Mexico

ESCAPE TO MEXICO

I WAS HAUNTED by the words of that old lover's lament, "You made me what I am today, I hope you're satisfied, you rascal-- you!" My ex-husband, Jerry, made me into what I am today; he stole my life. He was a sexual predator!

When I first met Jerry my sexual needs and actions were average for a 20-year-old girl, although I admit I had a natural talent for sexual fun. He manipulated me until I was what he wanted me to be. He disregarded what he was doing to my personal balance and adjustment to society. He made me obsessed with penises and taught me to seek them out, no matter the cost. He immersed me in sexual activity well beyond the imagination of the most sinful of church deacons.

Before I went to Jerry for counseling I liked my job and had an active interest in sports. I enjoyed spending evenings with other people my age. I went to bars for entertaining conversations, not just so I could hook up with a guy and end up in bed. I loved my apartment and liked decorating it. I even started putting together a modest layette in anticipation of eventually fulfilling my life with motherhood. I even liked staying home alone to do my hair and watch TV.

Jerry changed all that when I went to him for counseling. I became a recluse, concerned only with sexual gratification. We never went anywhere to have fun anymore. My perspective and focus became so distorted that I believed I was happy and had found the ideal life.

After Jerry went out of my life I had nothing left. All the usual leisure activities available to others were boring for me. Movies were no longer any fun without the customary blow job included. I had been turned into a weird person and I no longer had a place in the world. Jerry had stolen my life!

Jerry made me into such an insatiable slut that I was no longer able to teach school in the U.S. He brought me to ruin and made me a fugitive from American justice. He liked to please me and I admired him, but he had feet of clay

When Jerry finished with me he left me to face the consequences of his training. I had become so obsessed with the male penis that I could think of nothing else. I hated myself when I sought to gratify my needs by going outside the home. He gave up and deserted me, and let those two lecherous fathers of my students rape me.

You see before you a vivacious young woman disguised as a lad, who tries to live life to its fullest. I try to appear masculine so that I will have little attraction to males. God knows it's bad enough that I want men, without them desiring me, too. She summarized: You and your intolerant society have taught me to direct every sexual move to my own selfish benefit. I no longer have uninhibited orgasms; now I have calculated conclusions that benefit me. I have become a high-class whore.

* * * * *

After I escaped from the Georgia police I stopped over to visit my oldest sister in Miami. I didn't expect to get much help because we were always jealous of each other. Even as kids we never got along. These roots of my hostility in sibling rivalry became clear during my counseling sessions.

My sister was ready to give me a little bit of help, even if it was just to get rid of me. In talking, we came to the conclusion that I should go on the lam to Mexico. My sister offered me refuge until I could get my passport and other matters in order.

The time came to say good-bye after several weeks of ducking around in dark alleys. It was good-bye to Georgia, to Miami and to all the rest of the good old USA. I would never return.

I flew a little more than an hour and found myself in the paradise of the Mexican Caribbean. We landed on the island of Cozumel, famous for fun and old Mayan ruins. I had been to Mexico City before and liked it. I had expected to return some day to Mexico, but never like a dog with exploding firecrackers tied to its tail.

As I went through the immigration and customs lines, I felt like the criminal I was. I kept expecting to be pulled off the line for questioning. I had seen too many movies about criminals being stopped at the border crossings. I hardened my self so I would be able to endure apprehension and maybe even detention. I breezed through-- Thank God!

Nobody was expecting me, but Pedro was there with the other hustlers trying to catch any of the smaller fish that slipped through the larger nets cast by the tourism companies. Pedro was a free-lancer, who had seen lots of lost souls come and go through his heavenly island of Cozumel. He knew what they needed most, so he would provide them with a little food and lots of tequila. He had the right idea, "Save the soul, and the body will take care of itself."

All I did for the first few weeks was drink tequila and hang out in the sun. Pedro understood-- he waited patiently. After about a month he brought me back to reality and the needs of the day.

He asked me, "How do you expect to repay me for supporting you?" I was a good-looking chic and had a body to match so he knew he wasn't risking too much by supplying me with the necessities for survival. He figured he always could "take it out in trade" if he had to.

I wouldn't have minded "doing" Pedro. He was a swarthy, macho-looking Mexican of about 40. I took to him the first day, but he made it plain to me that he wasn't the sort of guy who plays around for the fun of it.

He admitted that his main interest in life was to acquire all the material goodies he could, with a minimal amount of exertion. He wasn't the sort, who would squire a girl just for the fun of it. He was too self-interested to disperse his sexual favors just to make his partner happy.

Pedro had a wife and seven children living on the mainland in the city of Playa del Carmen. He enjoyed going home to be with them when business didn't detain him. He was open and direct in his dealings with people, and obviously fun-loving.

He was a good man and easy to like. When we were by ourselves he was much quieter; I realized that much of his joviality and pleasantness was part of his persona to please the tourists.

He was serious about his family and they respected him. Every year he put aside the pursuit of material things so that he could visit his mother in a village outside Veracruz. He had to work hard to get his children an education in this semi-impoverished country.

I asked him, "Why do you have so many children?" He said, "It's a tradition to have more than four sons. Did you know that they even have an honorary title for us fathers? *Padre de mas de quatro.* He explained, "The fathers of the volunteers for the revolutionary army of Poncho Villa used to take pride when their sons would enlist. They would say, 'I am sorry I have only four sons to give to battle for our freedom.' "

He told me that he was a guide and a pimp, and asked me if I wanted to work for him. I apologized for not being a money-making whore, but assured him that I was ready to go along with his ideas as to how to earn money from the visitors to the island.

Pedro was honest but a good business man. He was always ready to give you his time or do you a favor. He was generous but he always expected something in return, and almost always received it. Pedro was an all-around nice guy!

Everybody in the city of Playa del Carmen knew Pedro and liked him. He was the *Caput Capitis* of the village-- the Head Godfather. In fact he was the baptismal godfather of more than 20 of the local residents. When asked about them he would become confused about their names because there were so many of them. Still, he always managed to send a name day present to each of them. Family was everything to Pedro; he warned me "Don't ever get caught ass-backward with my family-- they will always come first!"

* * * * *

I started paying for my stay in Cozumel by taking money for "escort services." At first I resisted men's sexual overtures, but sex was my whole life back in Atlanta. I still loved sex, so for some months I kept on living more like a call-girl than an escort. Pedro was my pimp at first but he became more like a protective friend as I cut back on my whoring.

In the first months I accepted assignments for partnering with other women. I didn't find them anywhere near as interesting as mates with penises. When I did find a girl looking for action, I would be eager to do her sexually. Then when it same down to performing, I would bemoan that she wasn't a guy with all the trimmings. I would reach down between her legs and find only soft, yielding flesh. Still, sex with women was much safer than with men.

I went on for many months appearing in public, looking like a transvestite. I employed my sharp razor-cut hair and fashionable pant suits to emphasize my masculine side so that I would attract women-- they would be safer than men.

I couldn't suppress my basic needs for very long, so I started wearing fluffy, long-hair wigs as chum to troll for men. I lived on a see-saw: A week of female partners; then there would be the switch to males. I vacillated between what was safe and good for me, and what I really wanted.

Eventually I met Berta, and she and I moved into my new beach house. Berta may not be very exciting but she makes me feel safe. She is good for me; she keeps me stable. Berta keeps me on the straight path when I become involved with men and lose control, and veer toward trouble. Thanks to her and Pedro I have never been busted by the local police.

But the power that the penis holds over me is undeniable. I should build one of those Indian religious shrines and place the largest dildo I can find in the center of it. Around it I could place penis-shaped candles to express my admiration for the "Great One." Dependable old Pedro visits me and lets me enjoy his physical charms about once a month. He is never demanding or rough. He is a very pleasant man and he keeps me happy. Without Pedro and Berta I would be out in the streets, giving it away. How fucked up can a person be?

* * * * *

My life in Mexico was good; the last thing I needed was a self-centered husband to screw it up. I swore I would never be dependent upon Jerry for anything from the day he deserted me and let me be raped.

That was not to say that I wouldn't mind having the opportunity to take advantage of him, just as he did with me. There were no immediate advantages to being his wife, but I remained civil with him. He even found his way into my bed, but I didn't come running; he had to beg me to submit. Now that he had surfaced I had my chance to make him pay for stealing my life.

DELAYED REWARDS

WE DIDN'T even know for sure the name of the attacker, who was choking Jerry to death before our very eyes. He had his nerve bringing his violence and hate into my house! Murder is not a sport that one engages in casually. He was well-dressed so I guessed that he was one of the family from Miami, or somebody they had sent over to kill Jerry.

Berta and I just sat frozen in our chairs. We couldn't believe what we were seeing-- Jerry was being chocked to death in our very own living room! At the beginning we didn't even have time to react; we just sat there immobilized. Finally, Berta screamed at the killer to stop, but he wasn't listening. Rage continued to distort his face. He no longer had any control and he was unable to come to his senses until Jerry lay stretched out dead on the floor.

By the time I recovered, I realized that we had become inconvenient witnesses. Would the two of us have to fight it out against this intruder? It looked like we would have to kill him or be killed by him.

As the killer recovered control he began shaking with emotion; it seemed like he was crying. Thank God! He was no cold-blooded killer-- maybe we could reason with him-- make some kind of a deal. When he spoke we were taken off balance because he started apologizing to us. I breathed a sigh of relief. No, we didn't excuse him; I didn't just say, "It's alright, things like that just happen sometimes!"

I begged him to just leave and take his dead friend with him. I reminded him that neither of us knew who he was, and that he would have time to leave the country before anybody would be looking for him. I managed a little smile, "See! Were really not witnesses-- right?"

He intentionally withheld his name. That was good; the less we knew about him the less our threat to him. He explained that he followed Jerry to our house to berate him, not to kill him. He swore, "I never meant to kill him, I just lost all control-- I went crazy."

Then his face softened as he addressed us, "I can pay you well for your help and silence, if you agree." He explained, "I brought 100 grand with me to hire a hit man to take a contract on this bastard's life, but I never found one. I'll give you all of it if you help me get rid of the body and keep quiet about this accident."

I asked him if it would be alright if I went to the kitchen to put some coffee on. He smiled a little as he said, "Why not? We're getting to be friends aren't we?" I was stalling for time and Berta knew it.

She came into the kitchen and we left the killer on the couch. Berta is no fool; she said, "He probably will kill us if we refuse to take the money to help him. We have no choice but to accept it and trust that he won't kill us." We really had no choice, no decision, to make.

We returned to the living room and I deliberately sat next to the killer as if we were friends. I turned my face toward him and said, "Of course we'll help you. Who wouldn't for that kind of money?" He was pleased; he understood the power of money.

He noticed that the back of our house fronted on a small tidal canal, and that we had a small fishing skiff moored to our little dock. We agreed that he would leave us and go to his hotel, while we would take the body out and hide it in the swamp. He asked us if the two of us could drag the body down to the dock and lift it into the boat without any help. We assured him that we could.

The killer was getting off too easily; we had no guarantee that he would pay us off before he left town. I insisted that he bring us the money before we dispose of the body. He implored us to do our part up front, but I stood firm. We wanted to have the corpse as evidence in case he didn't return with our payment. He said that there was no way he could get the money before the banks opened in the morning.

We were deadlocked, so I suggested that we just leave the corpse in a closet until he came back with the money, even though it wouldn't be until tomorrow morning. None of us were going anywhere until everything was settled, and nobody would be fussing around our house, let alone looking in our closet. He agreed, and helped us drag the body out of sight; then he bade us goodnight.

The killer was not very experienced at dealing with the law. If he were, he would have noticed that I followed him to his hotel. I wasn't taking chances that he might renege on the deal and just leave us with the body. I established his identity for $20.00 and went back home. The killer turned out to be Jerry's brother-in-law, Sheldon Cohen-- just what I was expecting.

An excited Berta greeted me at the door with a big embrace. We were rich! We opened a bottle of champagne.

I owned the house we lived in, a gift from Jerry. We would go ahead and rent out that one, and occupy and live in the house Jerry bought later to be near me. We also would have the rental income from the beach house I purchased from my divorce settlement. The money from the killer would permit us to buy a couple of small houses to produce income for us to live on. We eventually would have steady income from five houses. What started out as an ominous, threatening evening, not only brightened up, but became very rewarding!

The cash arrived by messenger the next forenoon. I presumed that the killer was too busy getting out of Dodge to deliver it himself. We couldn't move the body until night-time so we sat around watching old videos and keeping Jerry company while he rested in the closet. It was all pretty weird, but what else can you expect when you buy into a murder?

We found a couple of old concrete cinder blocks in the back yard. That evening we took them down to the boat along with a strong mooring rope. Then we put on our swimming suits. We took Jerry out of the closet and laid him on a small rug so that it would be easier to slide him along. We dragged him down to the dock and rolled him into the boat.

We let the tide carry us several hundred feet and then we entered the mangrove bushes by reaching out and pulling on the roots and branches sticking out of the water. We didn't have to go more than twenty feet inside to be sure that the body wouldn't be discovered. The thick mass of roots obscured all light-- we couldn't see anything. We even had to fasten the cement blocks to Jerry's waist by feeling, rather than seeing.

It was a big struggle to get back to the canal because the roots were all entwined. It had been difficult for us to enter the swamp at that point, so it would be unlikely that anyone else would stumble along the same track. We left the body behind to rot away, submerged in the mucky water of the jungle.

The burial was devoid of ceremony and decency-- just what Jerry deserved! Berta wanted us to say a prayer before leaving the corpse but I vetoed it. I said, "Now that my life has been restored to me I don't have to make deceitful gestures. I'm my own person once again! Fuck Jerry!"

We returned home without incident and washed down the boat with the hose that was attached to the little dock. Then the two of us went up to the house and, scrubbed each other in the shower. After that we gave each other a sexual treat. Next came another bottle of champagne to celebrate our new inheritance.

The following day we started transferring our possessions to Jerry's beach house, our new home. We would house-sit it for Jerry. If anybody got curious about the previous occupant of our new house, we would just tell them that he had moved back north and that we were taking care of it for him. We had used that story before and it worked fine for us.

* * * * *

We watched the Miami paper every day for news about Jerry's disappearance. Nothing appeared for all the first week, but then there was a small story about a missing corporation executive. He was named and described. The public was being asked to provide information to the Miami police. The paper gave only the simplest details:

"Jeremiah Gordon failed to report to his office for the past several days. His absence was noticed because there were important documents that needed his signature."

There was no indication in the newspaper that any of the family was worried about him. How sad to have people concerned about concluding business arrangements rather than being worried about your welfare!

Pedro continued to come around for a visit about once a month to keep in touch and assure himself that my needs were being met. When he found that we had moved into Jerry's beach house, he merely congratulated us, but didn't ask questions. Pedro was ready to accept other's secrets but he never pressed for them. He was a good friend to have at your back.

Order eventually returned. Berta and I never discussed the unpleasant mess we got into the night Jerry last visited us. We both pretended that nothing had happened, and that worked for us. Neither Berta nor I were the jealous type so we found little to quarrel about.

She wasn't too happy when I started up a group for male Yoga wanabes. She knew me all too well. She wasn't as much jealous as she was protective. She knew that I would go overboard once I got back into the world of men's sweaty bodies.

Of course she was right, and I lost my way after the first few weeks of drooling over those hot male bodies. It reached the point where I was doing a couple of guys a day without getting a whore's wages. The trouble was that I loved it.

My dependable friends, Berta and Pedro laid it out for me so that I would see that I couldn't continue on the way I was going. I used Pedro to set firm limits for me, and we were able to dissolve the group and return my life to normal.

Life settled down to the pace of a humdrum retirement. There wasn't much to do because everything was pitched to please tourists. I got bored and started giving Yoga classes at night to young women-- I knew better than to get mixed up again with men. Berta served as my teaching associate, and protector. She prevented me from getting too deeply involved with the students, but that doesn't mean that we didn't allow ourselves a few flings with some of the girls.

I had learned to control my youthful interests better. We continued to offer classes for several years-- until I became bored with it all. After that I entered the only period of my life when I wasn't constantly looking over my shoulder.

FIVE YEARS LATER

MY five-year-old son had interchangeable fathers. When he was newborn I knew that only Pedro or Jerry could be the father. Pedro already had seven children and didn't need any more. Besides, my little baby showed no signs of a nascent Mexican moustache and didn't steal the mid-wife's wedding ring off her finger when she was delivering him. So I placed Jerry's name on the birth certificate as the father, and there was no one to dispute it. I had a marriage license to back up the claim to my rights. I named the infant Jerry and that was that.

My little bastard would have to grow up without a father, but he would be better off than having Jerry around to misguide him. The only relatives that he knew were his Tia Berta and his Tio Pedro. We didn't need anybody else.

When Jerry reached the age of understanding, I told him that his father was a great man, "He was a Hedonist, and he wanted people to be free to do whatever they desired."

"Your father was a teacher and a great man. He wanted people to be completely free. The world still was not ready to let people do as they wished, so the governments stopped your father from spreading the freedom concept. Your father had to escape from the American trouble-makers and the Mexican's were in on the plot to silence him, too."

I had been telling lies so often during the last eight years that it became easier for me to lie to my son than to tell him the truth. I invented as I went along:

"Your father went into the Quintana Roo jungles to meet the indigenous people to learn the truth about their plight. As always, the Mexican government supported the large landowners.

Your father was trying to see that the peasants had enough land of their own to be able to farm. These powerful landowners took the direct method of stopping your father's mouth-- they stuffed it with mud and clay."

All that I told him was the usual Mexican political bullshit, but it still worked. If I told him the truth about his father he would never have believed it. How could anybody be expected to tell a child that his mother conspired in the murder of his father, and then left him to rot in a mangrove swamp?

* * * * *

Jerry's in-laws reported him missing a month after his death. Everybody just assumed that he left the country to avoid the wrath of the family and the justice of the law. Sheldon knew better, but had to keep his guilty knowledge to himself.

The family's filing of a missing person's report started the time clock ticking. Mexican law dealt specifically with adjudicating a missing person as deceased when there was no corpse. Five years must elapse before such a missing person could be declared dead. I never contacted the family but I stayed informed.

When the time period was complete I went to the Quintana Roo court and declared that I was the widow of the missing Jerry Gordon, and that I was the legitimate heir of all his assets. The court accepted my passport and marriage license as sufficient evidence to rule that my missing husband was dead from undetermined causes; so I became his heir.

They gave me clear title to the house he left behind in Playacar, the one we were living in the guise of caretakers. All the stock in his name was transferred to my bank and I would be assured of receiving all the dividends in the future.

I even had the nerve to demand that Jerry's monthly Social Security payments for a widow be sent to me in Mexico. The darlings at Social Security acknowledged my claims by sending me a big fat check for the accumulated five years that had not been disbursed.

But I didn't leave matters at that. I even petitioned Social Security to make payments to our orphaned son. Yeah! The assets Jerry let behind went a long way to make up for his having stolen my life.

Jerry's in-laws were not very happy to see the whorish competition come out on top. It wasn't as though the family was starving; they just instinctively fought anybody, who set himself against them and their company.

My lawyer reassured me that they couldn't do a damn thing to prevent me from inheriting everything owned by my husband, as well as the assets that were willed to me by Rebecca. There wasn't a thing the family could do because I was on the right side of the law; that is, if you ignore my secret involvement as Accessory After the Fact in a Murder.

Even Dragon Mart prospered. The $50,000 I invested five years earlier grew to be worth $250.000. After my death my son would have title by right of inheritance to all his father's property as well as mine.

Fortune was smiling on me for a change; it was about time! Now that I was set for life I should have been contented, but I had been badly damaged. Once you lose your innocence, your naïveté goes as well. Once you have seen the boogyman behind the door you trust no one. How can I be sure that little Jerry will be safe from being molested sexually?

Can I entrust him to Berta? Can I trust myself to passively watch him grow into manhood without intervening?

<<Sic Transit Mundi>>

MORE MUSINGS

CLEANLINESS
The woman who keeps a clean house,
hides her dirty underwear.

CONTENTMENT
Is to appreciate what you had, and what you have--
not what you might have had or what you could have
had!

GARLIC
You've heard the expression, "Eat lot's of garlic.
it keeps you healthy."
I figured out where it comes from…
If you eat a lot of Garlic, sick people will keep their
distance!

MOTHER
What a wasted life my mother had!
My father was always gone from home,
and I wasn't.

JUDGEMENT
By what a man doeth,
so shall he be judged.

FLEAS
My fleas gave dogs

GYMS
What do you call an all-male gym?
A ball room.

LONGEVITY
Another secret of my longevity is refusing to eat things that are good for you, like broccoli.

CHANGING THE WORLD
I really never wanted to change the world.
I only wanted to scratch a few of its itchy spots!

TRUST
If you can't trust a 94-tear old man, who can you trust?
Answer: A 95-year-old-man.

LYING
I'm a good liar.
I'm good at telling the truth too, but
I don't get much practice with it

LAUGH AT OTHERS
Don't judge a person as "bad" because he laughs at the foibles of others, as long as he laughs harder at his own.

THE BEAST
The sexual beast in us only impresses a small footprint, but casts a tremendous shadow over all our lives.

TITS
Breasts are there to keep us men focused, when we're listening to an otherwise boring woman.

HISTORY
I'm appalled at the loss of information when a person of importance dies.
His understandings and truths are relegated to the trash bin, labeled "History."

ABOUT THE AUTHOR

THE AUTHOR is Professor Emeritus in the Florida University System-- a clinical psychologist by training and a cultural anthropologist by interest. He writes under a facetious pseudonym because he wants to keep his personal life separate from his professional one. Finally, after twenty-five years retirement, he elected to write some novels sharing his varied experiences as background.

Eleven titles are available from Kindle, Amazon Books, and booksellers around the world. He declares that this will be his last novel-- "It's time to *really* retire!" After much pleading he agreed to write one last novel, "The Shrink Who Stole my Life."

He has lived in Baghdad and in Cairo and has made more than 70 trips to Latin America, including 25 to Mexico, and 15 to Turkey. He is married to a wife from Baghdad and made the pilgrimage to Mecca. His wonderful children still hang out near the nest and encourage him.

wilson@jonathanslow.com
Wilson@musingsfromanoldman.com

JONATHAN SLOW